Table of Cont

FOREWORD

Faulty nutrition plays a major role in causing the chronic diseases (heart disease, arthritis, diabetes, cancer) that plague our society. We are a population addicted to salt, refined sugar, saturated fat and disease laden animal products. Over the last century, eating trends in the U.S. have increased these negative nutritional products in our diets producing devastating health consequences. The drive to reduce these excesses and move toward a vegan - vegetarian approach (eliminating all animal and dairy products) is a direction that is timely and essential. The dramatic reduction and/or elimination of animal proteins, fats and refined carbohydrates, while increasing fiber rich complex carbohydrates, vegetable based proteins, fruits and vegetables, provides us with benefits that are continually reinforced by the best clinical and scientific information available.

However, our imaginations and choices are limited by the old ways we have been conditioned to do things. Even our sense of taste, and our appreciation of wholesome natural foods has been jaded and shortchanged by the refined and processed foods we are used to. So, any new approach often elicits feelings of threat and disturbance. But, with a little patience, and a small sense of adventure, new nutritional possibilities can open up and transform your life.

At the Regency House Spa, vegan nutrition is a crucial and powerful mainstay of our healthy living approach to healthcare. I am fortunate as a hygienic physician to work with a kitchen under the direction of Chef John Nowakowski. Chef John's extensive experience in food preparation encompasses the most innovative vegan approach that I have ever experienced in 20 years of nutritional practice in vegetarian health centers. Vibrant vegetarian nutrition involves so much of the energy of taste, colors, aromas and presentation. Chef John will take you on a culinary adventure using nature's bounty as a palette to paint artistic displays that excite the palate, eye and nose as well as nurture the body.

(continued)

FOREWORD *(Con't)*

Because of our addiction to salt, sugar and fat, people changing over to low fat vegetarian cuisine often complain about the blandness of wholesome vegan recipes. Chef John has truly solved this dilemma by combining a masterful use of whole vegetarian foods with a tasteful use of gentle herbs and spices. His recipes entertain and delight both the novice and long term vegetarian alike, making transition to better nutrition exciting and easy. His recipes are time tested, representing many hours of love and practice on thousands of spa guests, and will translate beautifully into your home kitchen environment.

Healthy nutrition isn't about deprivation or necessarily eating less. It's about eating well. So, embrace this fabulous opportunity to share Chef John's love and passion for food preparation, and let it lead you into the exciting world of vegan - vegetarian cuisine. The vitality and pleasure will be all yours. *Bon Appetit.*

Dr. Frank Sabatino
Health Director
Regency House Natural Health Spa

Special Thanks

To my loving mother Ann, who taught me how good healthy food can taste. Together with my Dad John A., they both have given the love and support, to help us get through the tough times.

To my Princess Di (Diane Dolphin), Kari and Ginger for coming into my life and making it complete.

To all of the wonderful guests at the Regency House Natural Health Spa. Your requests for our recipes, and your true appreciation for what we have accomplished at the spa, were a constant motivating factor in the creation of this book.

To Nick Dejnega, without your support this would have never been possible.

Special thanks to Drs. Frank Sabatino and James Meschino. Your enthusiastic support, guidance and education have enabled me to take this cuisine to the next level.

To Vinnie Chiarelli, without your photography expertise this could not have been possible.

To Dan Folleso, food stylist, your attention to detail is second to none.

To Ilse Gotsch and Rita Ringler for your passion for perfection in proof reading.

To Julio DiIorio, my recipe taste analyzer, confidant, marketing and design extraordinaire.

To Chefs Ken Hubscher and Debbie Fisher, for their delicious recipe contributions which made this endeavor more complete.

To Steve Meltzer and the staff at American National Printing, for your patience and dedication to excellence in the production of this book.

And finally, to my kitchen staff, who endured all of the changes that were necessary to create this exciting " Gourmet Vegetarian Cuisine " at the Spa.

John B. Nowakowski

John B. Nowakowski

Introduction

Everyone wants to know what has motivated me to take on the challenge of a Vegan Cookbook. The Vegan Cuisine is a lifestyle of the present and will provide ourselves and our children with a healthy, happier future. After spending the last 15 years in the high-pressured world of hotels and resorts as an Executive Chef, I also felt that a dietary and lifestyle change was necessary for me to enjoy a healthier life.

There are many wonderful vegetarian cookbooks available today. It seems like there is a new one coming out each month and for good reason. Surveys have shown that in the last 10 years, over 12 million Americans have taken on some form of a vegetarian lifestyle. With that taking place comes the ever increasing demand for continuing education about this lifestyle.

It is now possible to find organic produce and soy milk in the supermarket. The timing is right to make that healthy change without having to look too far for the products.

The main goal of this cookbook is to help you make the transition to a healthier, yet elegant way of cooking, with simple, easy-to-prepare techniques ! For those of you who have experienced the art of vegetarian cooking, you may also find that the recipes provided will give you new avenues to explore in this exciting cuisine.

For your convenience we have included a "Shopping Smart List" that can assist you in locating most of the items needed to produce the recipes in this book. The brand names listed will assist you in finding these items at your local natural food store.

In order to assist you with a well-rounded menu plan, there are 4 weeks of sample dinner menus and a basic lunch menu located in the back of the book. The sample menus are similar to our weekly programs at the spa. For those of you who have visited the spa, there should be a sense of comfort in knowing that you have already experienced the success of these dishes.

Vegetarian Cooking for Children in a fun and exciting manner is quite a challenge. In the Index there is an asterisk beside "Vegetarian Kid's Favorite Foods" recipes that have had wonderful results.

I certainly hope that my passion for food and pleasure can help you attain that level of good health and happiness we all wish to have.

Food Combining Made Simple

When you first visit The Regency House Health Spa, you may experience an initial shock. We recommend some rules of eating and food combining that will restructure your eating habits. The beauty of this situation is that with this shock comes a new-found knowledge of how we should be treating our bodies in the first place!

It will not take very long to understand the few basic foundations of our cuisine. Your mind will then trigger response and self-awareness that will make you more sensitive to the proper time for adequate digestion and able to make healthier choices in meal planning.

For your convenience and peace of mind when making decisions at meal time, we have listed below the simple rules to follow :

1. Avoid the drinking of any beverages, including water, 15-30 minutes before and after eating to allow for proper digestion.

2. When eating any of the melons in the melon family, do not combine with any other fruit or vegetable. Melons digest very quickly, usually in about 30 minutes. We do not want to interfere with this digestive process. Some melons of note are cantaloupe, honeydew, watermelon, casaba and crenshaw.

3. The same holds true for eating other fruits. Eat fruit alone. Do not eat any member of the melon group at that time.

4. However, leafy greens like Romaine lettuce, celery and cucumbers combine quite well with fruit and will help modify any unstable reactions you may have to the sugar content of the fruit.

5. Eat proteins and starches separately and combine them with salads and vegetables.

This rule becomes more important if you are eating animal protein. If, for example, you eat a piece of fish, do not eat it with rice or potatoes. Eat it with salad and cooked vegetables. Animal proteins will increase the sugar index of any carbohydrates you eat them with and will make it harder for you to lose weight.

6. We do not recommend coffee or decaffeinated coffee of any kind. There are wonderful coffees available made from roasted chicory leaves that will provide you with the aroma without the effects of caffeine. Consult our Shopping Smart List for brand name natural foods.

THE VEGETARIAN PYRAMID

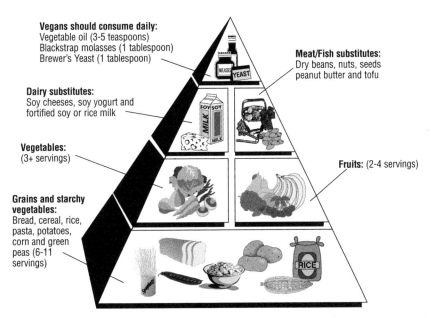

Vegans should consume daily:
Vegetable oil (3-5 teaspoons)
Blackstrap molasses (1 tablespoon)
Brewer's Yeast (1 tablespoon)

Meat/Fish substitutes:
Dry beans, nuts, seeds
peanut butter and tofu

Dairy substitutes:
Soy cheeses, soy yogurt and
fortified soy or rice milk

Vegetables:
(3+ servings)

Fruits: (2-4 servings)

Grains and starchy vegetables:
Bread, cereal, rice, pasta, potatoes, corn and green peas (6-11 servings)

GOOD HEALTH: The vegetarian pyramid recommends three or more servings a day of vegetables with a serving equal to half a cup cooked or chopped raw vegetables or one cup raw leafy vegetables.

VEGETARIAN FOOD PYRAMID: WHAT'S A SERVING?

Grains and Starchy Vegetables
■ **6 to 11 servings a day:**
1 slice bread (choose calcium-fortified bread if you don't consume dairy products)
1/2 roll or bagel
1 tortilla
1 ounce ready-to-eat cereal (vegans choose B-12 fortified cereal) or 1/2 cup cooked cereal, rice or pasta
3 to 4 crackers
3 cups popcorn
1/2 cup corn
1 medium potato
1/2 cup green peas

Meat/Fish Substitute
■ **2-3 servings a day:**
1 cup cooked dry beans, peas or lentils

1/2 cup shelled nuts
3/4 tablespoon peanut butter
3/4 tablespoon tahini
1/3 to 1/2 cup seeds
8 ounces bean curd or tofu, a source of calcium for those who don't consume dairy products

Dairy substitutes
■ **2 servings per day for adults, 3 for preteens, 4 for teens:**
1 cup calcium and vitamin D-fortified soy or rice milk if you don't consume dairy products)
1 1/2 ounces soy cheese

Fruits
■ **2 to 4 servings a day:**
1 medium hand-held piece of fruit
1/2 cup canned, chopped or

cooked fruit
3/4 cup fruit juice

Vegetables
■ **3 or more servings a day:**
1/2 cup cooked or chopped raw vegetables
1 cup raw leafy vegetables
3/4 cup vegetable juice

Plus for Vegans
3-5 teaspoons vegetable oil (for calories and essential fatty acid); vegans who don't include the fortified products suggested in the other food groups need 1 tablespoon blackstrap molasses (for iron and calcium) and 1 tablespoon brewer's yeast (for B vitamins, especially riboflavin; fortified brewer's yeast has B-12) or a vitamin supplement.

A Guide to "Shopping Smart"

For your convenience we have included a "healthy shopping list" to assist you in shopping smart at natural food stores as well as your local supermarket.

There are many enriched products on the market place today ranging from breads to pastas. The name brands provided are not enriched nor refined products. At the very least these products taste as good as any of the foods we have come to know and love. However, because the products have not been enriched with vitamins such as riboflavin, niacin or thiamine, it usually means that these products have retained its germ and fiber rich bran. This is turn makes it easier on our digestive tracks as well as more nutritionally sound.

The core of a vegetarian lifestyle is fruits and vegetables. We do suggest that you purchase organic products whenever possible. This will give much peace of mind knowing that food for your family has not been exposed to pesticides. If you cannot obtain organic produce, washing the produce before using takes on an added significance.

Produce Washing Procedure

Method 1.   Fill your sink with cold water, 4 tb. of sea salt and the juice of one lemon. Soak the fruits and vegetables for 5 - 10 minutes, then rinse in cool water and drain before using.

Method 2.   Use one teaspoon of clorox bleach to one gallon of cool water. Soak produce for 5 - 10 minutes, drain and soak in fresh water another 5 - 10 minutes. If there is a bleach odor, rinse again and allow product to air out before consuming.

Method 3.   To remove waxes, dip fruit in boiling water for 5 seconds. You may want to use tongs or grippers for safety.

*Now that we are better equipped to "shop smart",
the Vegetarian Magic in all of us will be alive and thrive !*

Shopping SMART Product List

Dairy Products   Brand

Egg Replacer for baking	Ener - G Foods Inc.
Rice Dream	Imagine Foods or Rice Milk by Westbrae
Westsoy Plus-Soy Milk	Westbrae Natural Foods
Almond Mylk	Wholesome & Hearty Foods
Silk-Soy Beverage	White Wave
Soy Cheeses	*Soya Kaas, White Wave or Soyco
Soy Parmesan Cheese	*Soyco "Light n Less" or Soymage
Soy Cream Cheeses	*Soya Kaas or White Wave
Soy Yogurt	White Wave Dairyless
Nonhydrogenated Margarine	Spectrum
Regular Tofu	Nasoya
Silken Tofu, 1% fat	Mori Nu
Tempeh	Light Life or White Wave
Egg Free Mayonnaise	Nayonnaise
Baked Italian or Flavored Tofu	White Wave
Soy Sour Cream	Soymage
Rice Sour Cream	Soyco

Organic Grains, Cereals & Pastas   Brand

Millet	Arrowhead Mills or Tree of Life
Legumes, Beans	Arrowhead Mills or Tree of Life
Brown Basmati Rice	Arrowhead Mills, Tree of Life or Lundberg
Oatmeal Flakes, Steel Cut Oats	Arrowhead Mills or Tree of Life
Pastas, (not enriched)	DeBoles
Lupin Pasta	IN-AG
Soba Noodles	Eden Foods or other
Amaranth Pasta	Health Valley
Quinoa (Keen - wa)	Ancient Harvest
Whole Wheat Couscous	Casbah or Fantastic Foods

* There may be trace amounts of casein, an animal protein necessary for the coagulation of quality soy cheeses.

Convenience Foods

Brand

Organic Tomato Products	Muir Glen
Pasta Sauces	Ci'Bella by Westbrae
Vegetarian Chilis	Hain or Health Valley
Mexican Salsa	Tree of Life
Salad Dressings	Blanchard & Blanchard or Ayla's Organics
Garden or Vegan Burgers	Wholesome and Hearty Foods
Boca Burgers	Boca Burger Trademark
Organic Frozen Pizzas	Soya Kaas
Frozen Meat Substitutes	Gimme Lean or Morningstar
Vegetarian Pepperoni Slices	Yves
Vegetarian Sliced Chicken or Turkey	White Wave

Condiments

Brand

Roasted Tahini	Arrowhead Mills or Joyva
Stone Ground Mustards	Westbrae Natural Foods or Hain
Brown Rice Syrup	Westbrae or Lundbergs
Barley Malt Syrup	Eden Foods
Coffee	Roma Coffee Substitute
Bragg Liquid Aminos	Braggs Brand (Replaces Tamari or Soy Sauce)
Herbal Teas	by Celestial Seasonings, Yogi or Traditional medicines
Sweetener & Fat Replacer	Fruit Source
Unrefined Sweetener	Sucanat
Low-Sodium Tamari	San-J
Cold-Pressed Olive Oil	Spectrum

If you are interested in our Shopping SMART video, call **(954)- 454-2220** and ask for the cookbook order department.

Appetizers and Salads

Clockwise from left, a "healthy" Caesar Salad, Black Bean and Corn Relish and Eggplant Caviar surrounded with Roasted Peppers, Artichoke Hearts and Hearts of Palm.

Angel Hair Pasta Pomodori Salad

This incredible salad is also excellent served hot.

12 oz.box	Whole Wheat or Durum Semolina Angel Hair Pasta
3 qts.	Distilled or Pure Water
4 each	Vine Ripe Tomatoes, chopped coarsely
1 tb.	Minced Garlic
1 tb.	Red Wine Vinegar or Balsamic Vinegar
1 bunch	Fresh Basil, chopped fine, reserve 1 sprig for garnish before chopping
1 tb.	Brown Rice Syrup or 1 ts. Sucanat
1/8 ts.	Cayenne Pepper
1/2 ts.	Sea Salt, optional
1 tb.	Organic Olive Oil, optional
2/3 cup	Soy Parmesan Cheese, "Lite n Less", by Soyco

Directions

1. Cook pasta 4-6 minutes in gently boiling water until al dente. (Tender, not soft)
2. Remove and strain in colander, rinse with cool running water and set aside.
3. Combine the next 8 ingredients in a mixing bowl.
4. In a large mixing bowl place the drained pasta and add the tomato mixture.
5. Fold in 3/4 of the parmesan cheese and chill .
6. Serve cold and garnish with a basil sprig and the remaining parmesan cheese.

Serves 4

Avocado and Tomato Salad with Lemon Dressing

Avocados are high in calories, but they are also very nutritional. They have been known to assist in the healing of ulcers. Eating tomatoes can reduce the risk of prostate illness.

Lemon Dressing

1/2 cup	Fresh Lemon Juice
1/4 cup	Distilled or Pure Water
1/4 cup	Olive Oil
1 tb.	Fresh Chopped Basil, Oregano or Cilantro
1/2 ts.	Sea Salt, optional
dash	Cayenne Pepper

Place all ingredients in a blender and puree.
Adjust seasonings to personal taste.

2 each	Ripe Avocados, cut in half, remove seed and scoop out with a spoon
2 each	Vine Ripe Tomatoes, cut into wedges or cherry tomatoes cut in half
1 each	Small Red or Vidalia Onion, cut in half and slice in 1/4 inch slices
1/3 cup	Imported or Ripe Black Olives

Directions

1. Cut avocado into 3/4 inch slices and place in a bowl with the remaining vegetables.
2. Toss the dressing with the vegetables, refrigerate until chilled and serve over fresh greens.

Serves 3 - 4

3

Baba Ganouche

This roasted eggplant dish is great as part of a salad or with pita crisps or crackers.

3 each	Eggplant, pierced several times with a fork
6 each	Large Garlic Cloves
1/3 cup	Sesame Tahini
1/4 cup	Fresh Lemon Juice
1/4 cup	Brown Rice Syrup (this will reduce any bitterness)
2 tb.	Stone Ground Mustard
2 tb.	Chopped Parsley
1 tb.	Bragg Liquid Aminos

Directions

1. Cut the top stem off the eggplant, then cut the eggplant in half lengthwise.
2. Preheat oven to 425 degrees. Place the eggplant and the garlic cloves on an oiled sheet pan (cut side down,) and roast approximately 45 minutes or until completely soft.
3. While the eggplant is roasting combine all other ingredients in a blender or food processor.
4. Place the roasted eggplant in strainer to let them drain and cool down.
5. Scoup out the pulp from the eggplant and process with the other ingredients.
6. Adjust seasonings and refrigerate until well chilled.

It may appear to be a small quantity at first;
however, the Baba Ganouche will expand as it cools.

Serves 4 - 6

Black Bean and Corn Relish

This is a wonderfully refreshing salad for a cookout or as an accompaniment to a Mexican entree.

2 cups	Cooked and seasoned Black Beans, reserve in a strainer
1 1/2 cups	Cooked Corn Kernels, from frozen
1 each	Red Pepper, diced 1/4 inch
1 each	Small Red Onion, diced
2 each	Vine Ripe Tomatoes, diced
1 tb.	Minced Garlic
1/2 bunch	Cilantro, chopped fine
1 each	Small Jalapeno Pepper, chopped very fine
2 tb.	Apple Cider Vinegar or Rice Vinegar
1 ts.	Sea Salt, optional

Directions

1. Combine all ingredients in a non-reactive bowl.
2. Adjust seasonings as needed and chill before serving.

Serves 4 - 6

If there is much leftover salad, try adding it to cooked brown rice for a Southwestern style rice.

Black Bean Hummus

By not using tahini, this is a very low-fat and flavorful hummus adaptation.

1 lb.	Organic Black Beans
2 qts.	Distilled Water
1 each	Medium Yellow Onion, 1/2" diced
1 each	Medium Red Pepper, 1/2" diced
2 tb.	Minced Garlic
1 tb.	Ground Cumin
1/4 ts.	Cayenne Pepper
1 ts.	Sea Salt
2 each	Bay Leaf
1/2 bunch	Cilantro, finely chopped
2 tb.	Bragg Liquid Aminos, optional

Directions

1. Soak black beans in cold water for 1-2 hours. Drain in colander.
2. Bring water to a boil , add beans and the next 7 ingredients.
3. Simmer 1 1/2 hours or until beans are tender.
4. Remove from stove and cool slightly.
5. Place the beans in a food processor or blender and add enough of the cooking liquid to puree into a smooth paste.
6. Remove and place into a bowl. Fold in the cilantro and Bragg, adjust seasonings as desired and refrigerate until cool.

Serves 6 - 8

Serve with raw vegetables, pita bread and your favorite salad items or with nacho chips and Mexican salsa.

Bowtie Pasta Salad
with Sundried Tomatoes

This dish was initially created with grilled shrimp, chicken breast slices or cajun scallops. It has adapted very easily to vegan style, simply by removing the animal products. I am sure you have favorite recipes that can still be enjoyed in much the same way.

12 oz.	Bowtie Pasta, a.k.a. Farfalle, if available tricolored bowtie pasta is even more colorful
2 qts.	Distilled or Pure Water
1/4 cup	Cold Pressed Virgin Olive Oil
1 tb.	Balsamic Vinegar
1/2 bunch	Fresh Basil Leaves
2 ts.	Minced Garlic
1/2 ts.	Sea Salt
1/8 ts.	Cayenne Pepper
2/3 cup	Sundried Tomatoes, softened in hot water and julienne
2 each	Vine Ripe Tomatoes, cut in wedges

Directions

1. Bring water to a boil, add pasta, stirring occasionally for 6-8 minutes until just tender. Strain in colander, rinse with cool water and strain again.
2. In a blender, puree the olive oil, vinegar and spices.
3. In a large bowl, toss together the pasta, tomato products and infused oil, adjust seasonings to taste.

Serves 3 - 4

This pasta may be served cold or heated and served hot as an entree. Garnish with basil sprigs.

Caesar Salad

I am most proud of this low-fat, low-sodium alternative to the original version. The balsamic vinegar gives it color and character, and the tofu lends its creaminess.

2 heads	Romaine Lettuce, cored, remove any brown spots
2 tb.	Fresh Lemon Juice
2 ts.	Minced Garlic
1 tb.	Stoneground Mustard, West Brae or Hain brands
2 tb.	Balsamic Vinegar
2 tb.	Distilled or Pure Water
1/4 lb.	Extra Firm Regular or Silken Tofu, drained, pressed and cubed
2 cups	Pita Croutons, located in Bread and Snacks chapter
1/2 cup	Soy Parmesan Cheese, "Lite n Less", by Soyco or Soymage

Directions

1. Clean Romaine and allow to crisp in the refrigerator for 1 hour.
2. In a blender add the next 5 ingredients and puree.
3. With the blender running, add the tofu until thickened.
4. Cut the romaine and toss with the desired amount of dressing. Garnish with pita croutons, and soy parmesan cheese.

Serves 6 - 8

Dressing will hold 5-7 days refrigerated.

Caesar Salad

Free of egg yolks, oil and anchovies, the low-sodium, cholesterol-free version of this classic will surprise you with its texture and flavor.

Creamy Cole Slaw

This cholesterol-free cole slaw will bring back memories of your favorite deli salad.

1 each	Small Green Cabbage, cut in half, remove core and slice very thinly or shred
1 each	Large Carrot, peeled if not organic and grated
1 cup	Shredded Red Cabbage (Optional for better color)
1 cup	Pineapple, peeled and diced into 1/2 inch cubes, optional

Cole Slaw Dressing

1/2 cup	Raw Apple Cider Vinegar
3/4 cup	Brown Rice Syrup
10 oz. box	Firm Silken Tofu, Low-Fat if available
2 tb.	Stone Ground Mustard
2 ts.	Celery Seeds
1/2 ts.	Sea Salt
dash	Cayenne Pepper

Directions

1. Prepare the vegetables and place in a large mixing bowl.
2. To prepare dressing, place all items in a blender and puree for 30 seconds.
   Adjust seasonings to your version of the correct sweet and sour flavor.
3. Toss the dressing with the cabbage, and chill, stirring occasionally.

Serves 6 - 8

Curried Couscous Salad

This is a very light salad that could also serve as a hot dinner entree.

1 1/2 cups	Whole Wheat or Durum Semolina Couscous
3 cups	Distilled or Pure Water
2 tb.	Curry Powder
1 ts.	Sea Salt
dash	Cayenne Pepper
3/4 cup	Raisins
1 each	Julienne Carrots, 1/4" x 1 1/2 "
3/4 cup	Snow Peas, cut on an angle (or Frozen Baby Peas)
1 each	Medium Red Pepper, diced 1/2"
2 each	Scallions, sliced 1/4 inch slices

Directions

1. Bring water to boil in a medium sauce pot, add spices.
2. Add raisins, snow peas and carrots.
3. When the stock is about ready to boil again, stir in couscous, cover with the lid and turn off heat.
4. Allow to sit covered 5-10 minutes, stirring occasionally. Add red peppers and scallions, chill, or serve hot.

Serves 4 - 6

For a nice change in flavor try adding fresh diced mango or papaya, walnuts, sundried cranberries or cherries, diced apples or cooked pink lentils.

Eggplant Caviar

This roasted eggplant, garlic and sundried tomato dish is a great addition to a salad. It also serves well as a tasty low-fat appetizer dip for crudites or pita crisps with imported olives.

2 each	Medium Eggplants, about 2 pounds
1 tb.	Organic Cold Pressed Extra Virgin Olive Oil
6 each	Large Garlic Cloves, peeled
1/2 cup	Finely chopped Sundried Tomatoes
3 tb.	Organic Tomato Puree (Muir Glen Brand)
1 tb.	Balsamic Vinegar
dash	Cayenne Pepper
1tb.	Braggs Liquid Aminos
1 tb.	Finely chopped Italian Parsley

Directions

1. Preheat oven to 450 degrees. Cut eggplant in half lengthwise, brush the cut side with olive oil, and place on sheet pan cut side down.
2. Place the garlic cloves in the same pan and also brush with olive oil.
3. Bake 40-45 minutes or until the eggplant is tender and the garlic is browned. Remove garlic cloves before they blacken.
4. Let the eggplant cool in a colander to drain and when cool, scoop out the pulp with a spoon.
5. Place all ingredients in a blender or food processor and blend together.
6. Adjust spices as desired and refrigerate until very cold.

Serves 4 - 6

Fat-Free Cucumber Dill Salad

This salad is especially colorful served on a bed of field greens or mesclun lettuce.

3 each	Large Cucumber, peeled and sliced into 1/4 inch slices
1 each	Medium Red Onion, cut in half, then into 1/4 inch slices
1/2 cup	Raw Apple Cider Vinegar
2/3 cup	Brown Rice Syrup
1/4 ts.	Sea Salt
dash	Cayenne Pepper
2 tb.	Fresh chopped Dill

Directions

1. Cut vegetables, toss together in a large bowl, and set aside.
2. For marinade, place the next 4 items in a blender and puree.
3. Toss vegetables with the dressing and dill and refrigerate.
   Adjust seasonings to your version of the correct sweet and sour flavor.
   Stir occasionally for better flavor distribution.

Serves 3 - 4

"Fire and Ice" Salad
(Marinated Tomatoes and Cucumbers)

This is a great " buffet type " salad, or
for a simple dinner salad serve over cut greens .

2 each	Vine Ripe Tomatoes, cored and cut into wedges
1 each	Large Cucumber, peeled and sliced into 1/4 inch slices
1 each	Medium Red Onion, cut in half, then into 1/4 inch slices
1/4 cup	Black Olives (Optional, if watching those fat calories)

Marinade

1/3 cup	Raw Apple Cider Vinegar
1 tb.	Canola Oil
1/2 cup	Brown Rice Syrup
2 ts.	Celery Seeds
1/2 ts.	Sea Salt
dash	Cayenne Pepper

Directions

1. Cut all vegetables and toss together in a large bowl.
2. For marinade, place all items in a blender and puree for 30 seconds.
   Adjust seasonings to your version of the correct sweet and sour flavor.
3. Toss vegetables with the dressing and chill, stirring occasionally.

Serves 4 - 6

Garbanzo Bean Hummus

This Middle Eastern appetizer dip can be served with pita bread and a salad.

3 cups	Cooked Garbanzo Beans, strain and reserve the liquid
1/3 cup	Tahini (Ground Sesame Seeds)
1/2 cup	Fresh squeezed Lemon Juice
2 tb.	Italian Parsley, finely chopped
2 tb.	Bragg Liquid Aminos
1 tb.	Minced Garlic
1 ts.	Ground Cumin
1/8 ts.	Cayenne Pepper

Directions

1. Blend all ingredients in a food processor or blender with some of the reserved liquid.
2. Add enough of the reserved juice from the garbanzo beans for proper consistency.
3. Adjust seasonings and refrigerate.

Yield is 1 quart.

For a different flavor and color dimension, try adding 2/3 cup of roasted red peppers to this recipe. Blend peppers in the food processor with the other ingredients.

Greek Pasta Salad

This flavorful pasta can also be served as a hot entree.

3 qts.	Distilled or Pure Water
1 lb.	Tri-colored Rotinni Pasta
1 bunch	Fresh Basil Leaves
1 tb.	Minced Garlic
1/2 cup	Organic Cold Pressed Olive Oil
1/2 ts.	Sea Salt
1/8 ts.	Cayenne Pepper
1 cup	Sundried Tomatoes, softened in scalded water and cut coarsely
1/2 cup	Black Olives, sliced
1/2 cup	Green Olives with Pimientos, sliced
1/3 cup	Grated Soy Parmesan Cheese, lite style

Directions

1. Bring water to a rolling boil, add pasta and stir frequently. Cook 6-8 minutes, or until just tender.
2. Place pasta in a colander and rinse quickly with cool water.
3. Combine next 5 ingredients in a blender for a superior consistency and flavor.
4. In a large mixing bowl toss pasta with the dressing and add the remaining ingredients.
5. Refrigerate until cool and garnish with soy parmesan cheese and a basil sprig.

Serves 4

Heart to Heart Salad
(Marinated Hearts of Palm and Artichokes)

Hearts of palm come from the cabbage palm tree. There is a festival every February in La Belle, Florida honoring this vegetable. (The old timers call it "swamp cabbage".)

1 can	Hearts of Palm, drained and sliced 1/2 inch thick on an angle
1 can	Artichoke Hearts, drained and cut in half
1 each	Small Red Pepper, cut into 1 inch cubes
1 each	Small Yellow or Orange Pepper cut into 1 inch cubes
1/3 cup	Ripe Black Olives, drained
1/3 cup	Green Olives, drained
8 each	Cherry tomatoes, cut in half, or
2 each	Vine Ripe Tomatoes, quartered, optional

Marinade

1/4 cup	Cold Pressed Virgin Olive Oil
1/4 cup	Raw Apple Cider Vinegar or Rice Vinegar
2 tb.	Fresh Lemon Juice
1 ts.	Minced Garlic
1/2 ts.	Sea Salt
1 tb.	Oregano Leaves
dash	Cayenne Pepper

Place all ingredients in a blender and puree for 30 seconds.

Directions

1. Cut all vegetables and toss with olives and marinade. Serve on a bed of greens.

Serves 4

Jicama Orange Salad

Jicama is a root vegetable, very popular in Central America. It resembles a turnip, but is slightly sweet with the flavor resembling an apple.

1 each	Jicama, peeled and julienne on a mandolin. If you do not have a mandolin you may julienne in 1/8 x 2 inch strips with a knife.
1 cup	Fresh Squeezed Orange Juice
2 tb.	Rice Vinegar
dash	Cayenne Pepper
2 tb.	Fresh Peppermint, chopped
3 each	Oranges , peel to the flesh and remove sections as you would a grapefruit, avoiding the thick membrane.

Directions

1. Place the cut jicama in a medium bowl.
2. Combine with the next 4 ingredients, blend with the jicama and marinate for 2 hours.
3. Fold in the orange sections and serve as is or on a bed of cut greens.

Garnish with the peppermint sprigs.

Serves 3-4

Curried Lentil Salad

This hearty salad is high in protein and could also be reheated as an entree.

3 qts.	Distilled or Pure Water
1 lb.	Organic Green or Pink Lentils
2 each	Bay Leaves
1 ts.	Sea Salt, optional
1 each	Medium Vidalia or Yellow Onion, diced 1/2 inch
1 each	Carrots, finely diced or shredded
2 each	Celery, diced 1/4 inch
2 tb.	Curry Powder
1/3 cup	Fresh Lemon Juice (about 3 lemons)
2 tb.	Chopped Parsley
2 tb.	Bragg Liquid Aminos
1 tb.	Minced Garlic
1/8 ts.	Cayenne Pepper

Directions

1. In a large pot, bring the water to a boil. In a strainer rinse the lentils, checking for stones.
2. Add lentils, bay leaf and salt to the pot, cover and simmer for about 30 minutes while stirring occasionally.
3. Skim the foam off of the stock and cook only until lentils are tender. Remove from heat.
4. Strain the lentils, mix with remaining ingredients, adjust seasonings to taste and chill.

Serves 4

Seaweed Cole Slaw

This is a much healthier and more colorful version than the traditional cole slaw. We serve it to complement our vegetable sushi rolls.

1 pkg.	Wakame, soak in scalding water for 15 minutes, strain, with tip of the knife remove thick membrane and julienne 1/2 inch the outer leaves
1/2 head	Green Cabbage, cored and sliced or shredded 1/4 inch thick or thinner if possible
3 stalks	Bok Choy, trim away green leaves and slice 1/8 inch slices
1 each	Large Carrot, peeled if not organic and shredded
1 each	Small Daikon, peeled and shredded
2 cups	Oriental Vinaigrette, recipe on page 69
2 tb.	Toasted Sesame Seeds, bake in a pan @ 400 degrees for 12-15 minutes or place in a saute pan on medium high heat and toast until browned, stirring occasionally.

Directions

1. Process all vegetables and toss with the vinaigrette and half of the sesame seeds.
2. Refrigerate until well chilled, garnish with the remaining sesame seeds. Salad should keep for up to 2 days.

Serves 4 - 6

Wakame is prepared from a large brown seaweed. Seaweed contains more minerals than do land plants.

Sicilian Pasta Salad

My original version of this salad contained feta cheese cubes. Up to this time there is not a soy feta cheese product available. Soy parmesan cheese will replace the feta and provides a nice complement.

3 qts.	Distilled Water
1 lb.	Tricolored Orzo or other pasta
1 bunch	Fresh Basil Leaves
2 ts.	Minced Garlic
1/3 cup	Organic Cold Pressed Olive Oil
2 tb.	Balsamic Vinegar
dash	Cayenne Pepper
3/4 cup	Sundried Tomatoes, softened and chopped coarse
1/3 cup	Black Olives, sliced
1/3 cup	Green Olives with Pimientos, sliced
1/4 cup	Capers
1/3 cup	Soy Parmesan Cheese

Directions

1. Bring water to a rolling boil, add pasta and stir frequently. Cook 6-8 minutes, or until tender.
2. Strain pasta in a colander and rinse with cold water and drain.
3. Combine next 5 ingredients in a blender for a superior consistency and flavor.
4. In a large mixing bowl toss pasta with the dressing and add the remaining ingredients.
5. Serve cold with a sprinkle of the soy parmesan cheese and a basil sprig garnish.

Serves 4 - 6

Tabbouleh

You may have seen this traditional Lebanese salad spelled or prepared differently. I enjoy the chick peas for added texture and protein.

1 cup	Organic Bulgur Wheat
2 cups	Distilled Water
2/3 cup	Cooked Organic Chick Peas, strained
2 tb.	Chopped Italian Parsley
1 tb.	Chopped Peppermint Leaves
1 tb.	Minced Garlic
1 each	Vine Ripe Tomato, diced
1/3 cup	Fresh Lemon Juice
1 each	Small Red Onion, diced
2 tb.	Bragg Liquid Aminos
dash	Cayenne Pepper

Directions

1. Bring water to a boil, stir in the bulgur wheat, turn off heat and cover for 15 minutes, stirring from time to time until water evaporates.
2. Place the cooked bulgur wheat in a bowl and chill while preparing the other vegetables.
3. Combine all remaining ingredients with the bulgur, adjust seasonings as needed.

Serve well chilled.

Serves 4

Soba Noodle Salad
with Oriental Vegetables

Soba noodles are made from buckwheat and sometimes whole-wheat flour.
They cook like regular pasta and are a valuable source of protein.

12 oz.	Soba Noodles, cooked until just tender, rinse with cool water and chill
2 cups	Broccoli Florettes
2 each	Organic Carrots, sliced on an angle into 1/4 inch slices
1 cup	Snow Peas, remove stems and slice on an angle into 1 inch slices
4 each	Scallions, slice into 1/4 inch slices
1 can	Sliced Water Chestnuts, drained
1 can	Sliced Bamboo Shoots, drained
1 1/2 cups	Oriental Vinaigrette, recipe on page 69
2 tb.	Toasted Sesame Seeds

Directions

1. Cook or steam the broccoli, carrots and snow peas until just tender, then chill.
2. In a large bowl, toss the soba noodles, vegetables and remaining ingredients.
3. Refrigerate until cool, tossing from time to time to incorporate the flavors.

Garnish with toasted sesame seeds and serve.

Serves 4 - 6

Three Bean Salad

Try to use fresh cut beans with this old favorite and you will never use frozen or canned again .

1/2 lb.	Fresh Green Beans, trimmed and cut into 1 1/2 inch pieces
1/2 lb.	Fresh Wax Beans, trimmed and cut into 1 1/2 inch pieces
2 cups	Cooked Organic Kidney Beans, drained
1 each	Medium Red Onion, diced 1/2 inch
1 each	Red Pepper, diced 1/2 inch

Marinade

1/3 cup	Raw Apple Cider Vinegar
2 tb.	Canola Oil
1/2 cup	Brown Rice Syrup
1/2 ts.	Sea Salt
dash	Cayenne Pepper

Directions

1. Cut the beans, cook or steam 10-12 minutes until tender. Chill and toss together in a large bowl.
2. For marinade, place all items in a blender and puree for 30 seconds.
   Adjust seasonings to your version of the correct sweet and sour flavor.
3. Combine all vegetables with the dressing and chill, stirring occasionally.

Serves 4 - 6

Vine Ripe Tomatoes and Soy Mozzarella with Pesto

This is one of the most popular appetizers at the Spa. It can also be served as an entree salad.

1 head	Romaine Lettuce, rinse, core and allow to drain in refrigerator
3 each	Large Vine Ripe Tomatoes, slice into 1/2 inch slices
1 each	Medium Red or Vidalia Onion, thinly sliced
6 oz.	Regular Soy Mozzarella Cheese, Soya Kaas brand, slice into 1/8 inch slices
3/4 cup	Pesto Sauce, recipe on page 202

Directions

1. Line a flat salad plate with the crispy hearts of romaine.
2. Place over lettuce alternately a slice of tomato followed by a slice of onion 3 times.
3. Place 3 slices of soy mozzarella cheese over the tomatoes and onions.
4. With a tablespoon drizzle a spoonful or two of the pesto sauce over the salad and serve.

Serves up to 4

You may also substitute baby lettuce blends for the romaine for added color and variety.

Grilled Vegetable Salad

We created this salad as a means for using our leftover grilled vegetables from dinner. What we didn't know was how incredibly tasty it would be!

1 each	Eggplant, cut in 1/2 inch slices with skin on
2 each	Yellow Squash, cut on an angle into 1/2 inch slices
2 each	Zucchini, cut on an angle into 1/2 inch slices
3 each	Portabella Mushrooms, remove stem and scrape off the gills on the underside
2 each	Roasted Red Peppers, sliced into 1/2 inch slices, recipe in vegetable chapter

Prepare all vegetables and place in a large pan and set aside.

Marinade

1/2 cup	Canola Oil
1 ts.	Minced Garlic
1 each	Small Red Pepper, cut in chunks
2 ts.	Oregano Leaves
1 ts.	Rosemary or Thyme Leaves
1/4 ts.	Sea Salt
dash	Cayenne Pepper

Place all ingredients in a blender and puree to emulsify all the flavors.

Directions

1. Turn Bar-B-Que grill to its highest setting for 5 minutes or until very hot.
2. Brush the marinade over the cut vegetables and place brushed side down on the grill.
3. While the vegetables are grilling, brush the top of them with more of the marinade.
4. When dark grill marks appear on one side, flip over and repeat on the other side.
5. Place all grilled vegetables in the refrigerator until cool.

Grilled Vegetable Salad - *continued*

Salad Dressing

1/4 cup	Virgin Olive Oil
1 tb.	Bragg Liquid Aminos
2 tb.	Distilled or Pure Water
2 tb.	Fresh Lemon Juice
1 tb.	Balsamic Vinegar
1 tb.	Fresh chopped herbs...basil, oregano or tarragon or any of your favorite fresh herbs. Dry herbs will do in a pinch.
1 ts.	Fresh Minced Garlic
dash	Cayenne Pepper

Place all ingredients in a blender and puree or whip rapidly by hand until well blended.

Directions

1. Remove chilled vegetables from the refrigerator and cut in 3/4 inch thick slices.
2. Toss the vegetables lightly with the dressing, refrigerate for 1-2 hours and serve.

Serves 4 - 6

"Low-Fat" Waldorf Salad

*Substituting a non-dairy mayonnaise or a flavorful yogurt dressing
transforms this classic into a healthier alternative.*

3 each	Red Delicious Apples, cored and diced 1/2 inch
3 each	Granny Smith Apples, diced 1/2 inch or a combination of apples and D'Anjou Pears, cored and diced 1/2 inch
1/3 cup	Lemon Juice
3 each	Celery Stalks, diced 1/4 inch
1 cup	Red or Green Seedless Grapes
1 cup	Raisins
3/4 cup	Walnut Pieces
1 cup	Nayonnaise , *a silken tofu mayonnaise substitute or for a lower fat version try adding 1 1/2 cups of*

*Citrus Poppy Seed Dressing, Orange Honey Yogurt, Passion Fruit, Banana,
Strawberry or Guava Yogurt Dressings, located in the dressings chapter*

Directions

1. Cut apples, place in a large bowl and toss with lemon juice to prevent discoloring.
2. Add remaining ingredients and serve well chilled.

Serves 4 - 6

White Bean & Pesto Salad

This hearty salad is bursting with color and flavor.

2 1/2 qts.	Distilled or Pure Water
1 lb.	Organic Navy Beans or Great Northern Beans
2 each	Bay Leaves
1/8 ts.	Cayenne Pepper
1 cup	Pesto Sauce, recipe on page 202
1 each	Red Pepper, diced 1/4 inch
1 bunch	Scallions, sliced 1/4 inch

Directions

1. Soak beans in scalding water for 1-2 hours. Bring distilled water to a boil.
2. Drain the beans and add to boiling water with the bay leaves. Cook for 1 hour or until beans are tender.
3. While beans are cooking prepare the pesto sauce and remaining vegetables.
4. When beans are tender, remove and drain in a colander.
5. Chill the beans, then fold in the pesto sauce and remaining ingredients. Allow to marinate for 1/2 hour or more to maximize flavors.

Serves 4-6

Marinated Wild Mushroom Salad

Portabella Mushrooms make this a very hearty salad. If availability is a problem, you may also use domestic mushrooms.

4 each	Portabella Mushrooms, destemmed, scoop out the gills on the underside of the cap with a spoon, rinse well and cut into 1/4 inch slices
	or 2 lb. Domestic Mushrooms, cut in half and rinsed well
1 tb.	Cold Pressed Virgin Olive Oil
1 each	Yellow Onion, diced 1/2 inch
1 tb.	Minced Garlic
1/3 cup	Balsamic Vinegar or Raw Apple Cider Vinegar
2 ts.	Thyme or Tarragon Leaves
1 each	Bay Leave
1/2 ts.	Sea Salt
dash	Cayenne Pepper

Directions

1. In a wok or large saute pan heat olive oil and saute the onions.
2. When the onions have slightly browned, add the garlic and brown lightly.
3. Add the vinegar, mushrooms, cover and continue to cook.
4. Add the remaining herbs and spices, cover and simmer until the mushrooms are tender.
5. Adjust seasoning if necessary and refrigerate until well chilled.

Serves 3 - 4

Herbed Wild Rice Salad

A grass native to the Great Lakes region of North America, wild rice is a distant cousin of common rice. Although expensive, it is rich in protein and carbohydrates.

1 1/2 qts.	Distilled Water
1 1/2 cups	Wild Rice or Wild Rice Blends
1 each	Large Vine Ripe Tomato, diced 1/2 inch
1 each	Cucumber, peeled, seeded amd diced 1/2 inch
1 each	Red, Yellow or Orange Pepper, diced 1/2 inch
1 each	Small Red Onion, diced 1/2 inch
3 each	Scallions, sliced 1/4 inch

Dressing

1/4 cup	Cold Pressed Virgin Olive Oil
2 tb.	Bragg Liquid Aminos
2 tb.	Fresh Lemon Juice
2 ts.	Minced Garlic
1/2 bunch	Basil Leaves
dash	Cayenne Pepper

Puree all ingredients in a blender.

Directions

1. Bring water to a boil and cook rice covered 40-45 minutes or until very tender and the rice has begun to split. Drain rice in strainer and refrigerate to cool.
2. Prepare all the vegetables and the dressing while the rice is cooking.
3. When rice is cool, toss with the vegetables and dressing and serve cold.

Serves 4 - 6

Wild Rice Salad
with Raspberry Dressing

You actually want to overcook the rice until it splits
for better texture in this salad.

1 cup	Wild Rice
1 qt.	Distilled Water
1 cup	Raspberry Vinaigrette Dressing, recipe on page 71
2 tb.	Poppyseeds (Optional)
1/3 cup	Sundried Cranberries
1/3 cup	Sundried Cherries
1/4 cup	Toasted Almond Slices

Raisins are a nice option if cranberries are unavailable.

Directions

1. Bring the distilled water to a boil and add the wild rice.
2. Cook the rice about 40 - 45 minutes until tender and there is splitting of the grain. Strain the rice and cool in the refrigerator.
3. While the rice is cooling prepare the dressing and toast the almonds.
4. When the rice is cool add all remaining ingredients and serve cold.

Serves 4

Soups

Clockwise from left, Black and White Bean Soup
Mexican Tortilla Soup and Spring Vegetable Soup.

Black Bean Soup

What would a South Florida cookbook be without a Black Bean Soup recipe? This recipe is also a lower fat version of the Cuban classic.

2 1/2 qts.	Distilled or Pure Water
1 lb.	Organic Black Beans
2 each	Bay Leaves
2 tb.	Minced Garlic
1 each	Large Yellow Onion, diced 1/2"
1 each	Red Pepper, diced 1/2"
2 tb.	Ground Cumin
1 bunch	Cilantro, finely chopped
1/4 ts.	Cayenne Pepper
1 tb.	Sea Salt (Optional)
1 piece	Kombu, 2 inch piece or 1 ts. Kombu Flakes

Soaking the beans for an hour or more will aid in reducing some of the gas effects of all beans. Beans cook faster and digest and taste even better when a small piece of Kombu is added. Kombu is a sea vegetable that is high in B vitamins, and iron. It is good for high blood pressure, cleanses the colon, aids the kidneys and anemia. Kombu can be found in Oriental or health food stores and comes in stiff, broad strands or in more-convenient-to-use flakes.

Directions

1. Soak black beans in scalding water for 2 hours. Bring distilled water to a boil.
2. Drain the black beans and add to boiling water with the bay leaves and kombu. Cook for 1 hour.
3. Add all remaining ingredients and cook until tender, about 1 1/2 hours more.
4. Adjust seasonings as needed and garnish with diced onion and cilantro.
5. For a creamier texture remove bay leaf, place soup in blender, cover tightly and puree.

Serves 4-6

If there are leftovers, do not despair. You can drain the beans and follow the recipe for Black Bean and Corn Relish or you may remove the bay leaf and puree to make a low fat Black Bean Hummus! For a complete dinner protein you may also combine it with brown rice to make Black Beans and Rice!

Cream of Broccoli Soup

The cream soups in this chapter are "naturally thickened" with potatoes and the main vegetable contained in the recipe. Say good-bye to the flour, butter and cream as well as the cholesterol and fats that went along with them in most "cream-style" soups.

1 qt.	Distilled or Pure Water
1 each	Large Yellow Onion, peeled, halved and sliced
3 each	Idaho Potato, peeled and quartered
1 each	Head of Broccoli, remove leaves and bottom half of stalk
1 tb.	Minced Garlic
dash	Cayenne Pepper
2 ts.	Sea Salt (Optional)
2 cups	Rice Dream or Soy Milk

Directions

1. Bring water to a boil.
2. Add onion and potatoes and simmer until potatoes are tender, about 20 minutes.
3. Meanwhile, cut broccoli into 1 1/2 inch pieces. Add to the stock with the garlic and spices and cook until just tender.
   (Do not overcook the broccoli or it will turn the soup to a brownish color.)
4. When broccoli is tender add the rice dream and remove from heat.
5. Place half of the soup in a blender or food processor and puree. Be sure to cover the blender securely or you can get burned. Remove from blender and return to the pot. Puree the remaining soup and season to taste.
6. To serve, reheat the soup slowly to desired temperature but do not boil.

Serves 6 - 8

For variety, add grated fat-free soy cheddar, jack or mozzarella cheese before serving. To create a different cream soup other than broccoli, try substituting celery, mushrooms, asparagus, or whatever vegetable favorite is available.

Cream of Carrot Soup with Dill

The sweetness of the carrots, to a large degree, will be responsible for the character of this soup.

1 qt.	Distilled or Pure Water
1 lb.	Organic Carrots, scrubbed and cut into chunks
1 each	Sweet Potato, peel and cut in 1/2 inch pieces
1 each	Medium Vidalia Onion or other, peeled, cut in quarters
1/2 ts.	Ground Nutmeg
1 ts.	Ground Cinnamon
dash	Cayenne Pepper
1 cup	Rice Dream, Soy Milk or Silk Milk
2 tb.	Freshly chopped Dill
1 ts.	Sea Salt (Optional)

Directions

1. Bring water to a boil and add the first 6 ingredients.
2. Simmer until the carrots are tender, then add the Rice Dream.
3. Puree the vegetable mix in a blender and return to the pot.
4. Reduce heat to low and fold in the fresh dill, adjust seasonings as desired and serve hot or cold.

Serves 6 - 8

Cream of Cauliflower Soup

The velvety texture of this soup will keep you coming back for more!

1 qt.	Distilled or Pure Water
2 each	Idaho Potatoes, peeled and sliced into 2 inch chunks
1 each	Large Vidalia Onion or other, peeled, cut in half and 3/4 inch slices
dash	Cayenne Pepper
1 ts.	Sea Salt
1 qt.	Cauliflower, cored, destemmed and cut into chunks
1 tb.	Minced Garlic
1 cup	Rice Dream or Soy Milk
2 tb.	Freshly chopped Dill (Optional)
4 oz.	Grated Fat-Free Soy Cheddar, Mozzarella or Monterey Jack Cheese (Optional)

Directions

1. Bring water to a boil and add the first 4 ingredients. Cook 20 minutes or until potatoes are tender.
2. Add the cauliflower and garlic, cover and simmer 10-15 minutes until the cauliflower is tender.
3. Add Rice Dream, remove from stove and puree the vegetable mix in a blender and return to the pot. Adjust spices as desired.
4. Reduce heat to low and fold in the fresh dill or cheese and serve hot or cold.

Serves 6 - 8

Lousiana Corn Chowder

The original recipe included backfin crab or crawfish meat.
Here is the vegetarian version.

1 quart	Distilled or Pure Water
3 each	Idaho Potatoes, peeled and cut into 2 inch slices
1 each	Large Yellow Onion , diced 1/2 inch squares
2 ts.	Sea Salt
4 each	Red Potatoes, scrubbed and cut into 1 inch squares, with the skin on, boil for 10 minutes, drain and set aside
1 cup	Rice Dream or Soy Milk
2 cups	Frozen Corn
1 each	Large Red Pepper, diced into 1/2 inch squares
1 tb.	Minced Garlic
1 tb.	Cajun Spice or 1 teaspoon Cayenne Pepper
1 tb.	Freshly chopped Chives (Optional)

Directions

1. Bring water to boil, add the potatoes and onions. Cook 20 minutes or until the potatoes are tender.
2. Place the cooked vegetables and stock in a blender, puree and return to the stove.
3. Add the red potatoes, rice dream, corn, vegetables and spices. Cover and cook until the red potatoes are tender.
4. Lower heat, adjust the seasonings and serve hot with the chive garnish.

Serves 6 - 8

Fabulous 5 Bean Soup

This entree style soup is truly a meal in itself. No need to make dinner if this soup is in your menu plans. It is so good that most guests request a second helping, thereby negating any need for another dinner course.

3 qts.	Distilled or Pure Water	2 each	Large Yellow Onion, diced 1/2"
1/2 cup	Organic Garbanzo Beans	2 each	Carrots, diced 1/2 inch
1/2 cup	Organic Kidney Beans	2 each	Celery Stalks, sliced 1/2 inch
1/2 cup	Organic Lima Beans	16 oz. can	Organic diced Tomatoes
1/2 cup	Organic Navy or	2 tb.	Thyme Leaves
	Great Northern Beans	2 tb.	Fresh Basil, chopped
1/2 cup	Organic Black Beans	1 tb.	Fresh Oregano, chopped
3 each	Bay Leaves	1/8 ts.	Cayenne Pepper
1 each	Kombu, 2 inch strip, optional	1 tb.	Sea Salt (Optional)
		2 tb.	Minced Garlic

Soaking the beans for an hour or more will aid in reducing some of the gas effects of all beans. Beans cook faster and digest and taste even better when a small piece of Kombu is added. Kombu is a sea vegetable that is high in B vitamins, and iron. It is good for high blood pressure, cleanses the colon, aids the kidneys and anemia. Kombu can be found in Oriental or health food stores and comes in stiff broad strands or in more convenient to use flakes.

Directions

1. Soak beans separately in scalding water for 1-2 hours. Bring distilled water to a boil in a large pot.
2. Drain the garbanzo and kidney beans, add to boiling water with the bay leaves and Kombu and cook for 30 minutes. Do not boil too rapidly or the kidney beans may split.
3. Drain the remaining soaking beans, add and cook for 30 minutes.
4. Add all vegetables and cook for 30 minutes, while stirring occasionally.
5. Add all spices, lower heat and simmer for 30 minutes or until beans are tender. Remove Kombu, cut into small pieces and return to the soup.
6. Adjust seasonings as desired. If soup is too thick for your liking add more water.

Serves 6 - 8

French Onion Soup

This recipe will rival any of your favorite onion soup recipes found in the finest restaurants. However, this one is also free of butter, dairy cheeses, animal based broths, and enriched flour that are often used to thicken the soup.

1 tb.	Canola Oil
3 each	Large Yellow Onions, peeled, cut in half and slice into 1/4 inch slices
3 tb.	Whole-Grain Flour
1 1/2 qts.	Distilled or Pure Water
1 each	Large Bay Leaf
2 tb.	Vegetable Protein Soup Base, Dr. Bonners or Jensens Brand or Low-Sodium Tamari
2 ts.	Sea Salt, optional
dash	Cayenne Pepper
4 each	Parmesan Crusted Crouton, recipe on page 209

Directions

1. Heat the oil on medium high in a large pot with a wide base. Now add the onions. Do not stir the onions until they have well browned on one side. You must resist the urge to stir the onions before they brown. This carmelization process will add to the sweetness as well as the color of the soup. Once browned, stir and continue cooking.
2. When the onions have browned evenly, lower the heat to warm and sprinkle in the whole grain flour. You must sprinkle the flour to avoid lumps in the soup.
3. Raise heat to medium high and stir in the water with a whip.
4. Add remaining ingredients and stir occasionally on a low boil for 20-30 minutes.

Adjust spices to taste and garnish with a parmesan-crusted whole wheat crouton.

Garden Vegetable Soup

Most soups that we have enjoyed in the past have been obstructed with high sodium chicken or beef bases. We can fully appreciate the distinctive flavors that each vegetable provides our soup recipes without the sodium powered soup bases. Most vegetable bases in supermarkets contain MSG. There are healthier soup bases available in natural food stores.

2 qts.	Distilled or Pure Water
12 oz.can	Muir Glen Organic Diced Tomatoes
2 each	Large Yellow Onion, diced 1/2 inch
2 each	Organic Carrots, 1/2 inch dice
2 each	Celery Stalks, 1/2 inch dice
2 cups	Green Cabbage, cored and diced into 1 inch cubes
2 each	Large Bay Leaf
2 tb.	Minced Garlic
1 tb.	Sea Salt (Optional)
1/8 ts.	Cayenne Pepper
1/2 lb.	Cut Green Beans
1 cup	Fresh cut or frozen Yellow Corn

Directions

1. In a large pot bring the water to a boil and add the next 9 ingredients.
2. Simmer vegetables for 20 minutes or until carrots are tender.
3. Add corn and green beans and cook 10-15 minutes until tender.
4. Season to taste and serve hot.

Serves 6-8

Chinese "Hot n Sour" Soup

As the name implies, this is a spicy soup. Feel free to change the amount of vinegar and chili paste to suit your personal tastes.

3 cups	Distilled or Pure Water
2/3 cup	Rice Vinegar or White Vinegar
2 tb.	Szechuan or Thai Chili Paste, dissolve with the vinegar
1/2 cup	Low Sodium Tamari or Shoyu, available in natural food and Oriental stores
1/2 cup	Arrowroot (it works the same as corn starch)
1 can	Bamboo Shoots, drained and diced 1/2 inch
1 can	Chinese Straw or Button Mushrooms, drained
1 cup	Diced Bok Choy, with the green leaves trimmed away
6 oz.	Firm Tofu, drained, pressed and cut into 1/2 inch cubes
1 bunch	Scallions, 1/4 inch slices
1 ts.	Sea Salt (optional)

Directions

1. In a large pot bring the first 4 ingredients to a boil.
2. Add 2/3 cup cool water to the arrowroot to make a paste and whip into the soup, lower heat and stir while soup thickens.
3. Adjust seasonings and thickness of the soup as necessary and fold in the remaining ingredients. Simmer for 5 minutes and serve hot.

Serves 4 - 6

Tamari and Shoyu are naturally fermented sauces derived from soybeans. Most soy sauces found in supermarkets are chemically processed.

Bavarian Lentil Soup

This is a nice hearty soup, high in protein and could also serve as an entree.

3 qts.	Distilled or Pure Water
1 lb.	Organic Green or Pink Lentils
1 each	Large Vidalia or Yellow Onion, diced 1/2 inch
2 each	Carrots, diced
3 each	Celery, diced
2 each	Bay Leaves
2 tb.	Minced Garlic
1 tb.	Sea Salt or 1/4 cup Bragg Liquid Aminos
1 tb.	Curry Powder
1/4 ts.	Cayenne Pepper

Directions

1. In a large pot, bring the water to a boil. In a strainer rinse the lentils, checking for stones.
2. Add lentils, cover and simmer for about 30 minutes while stirring occasionally.
3. Skim the foam off of the stock and add the vegetables and spices.
4. Continue to cook, skimming the foam as needed, and stirring often to avoid scorching.
5. When lentils are mushy and the soup has thickened as a result, adjust spices and serve.

Garnish with sliced Tofu Hot Dogs.

Serves 4 - 6

Mexican Tortilla Soup

This flavorful soup is a perfect start to a Mexican theme lunch or dinner.

1 tb.	Canola or Olive Oil
1 each	Large Vidalia or Yellow Onion
1 tb.	Minced Garlic
1 each	Yellow Pepper, diced 1/2 inch
1 each	Red Pepper, diced 1/2 inch
2 each	Vine Ripe Tomatoes, diced 1/2 inch
6 each	Tomatillos diced 1/2 inch (if available)
1 1/2 qts.	Vegetable Broth or Pure or Distilled Water
1/4 cup	Low Sodium Tamari or Soy Sauce
1 each	Bay Leaf
1 ts.	Ground Cumin
4 each	Corn on the Cob, cut the corn from the cob (or use 1 cup frozen cut corn)
1 each	Jalapeno Pepper, finely chopped
1 tb.	Fresh Oregano, chopped
2 tb.	Fresh Basil or Cilantro, chopped
3 each	Yellow or Blue Corn Tortillas, cut in half and julienne into 1/4 inch strips

Directions

1. Heat olive oil in a large pot and saute onions and garlic.
2. Add the peppers and tomatoes and simmer for 10-15 minutes.
3. Add the water, tamari and corn and continue to cook for 20 minutes.
4. While the soup is cooking, preheat oven to 400 degrees. Spread the cut tortillas on a sheet pan and bake for 20-25 minutes or until lightly golden browned and crispy.
5. Add the fresh herbs to the soup, adjust spices as desired and serve hot with the crispy tortilla chips as a garnish.

Serves 4 - 6

Tomatillos are Mexican green tomatoes that are small and pungent in flavor. They are not an unripened tomato. Tomatillos are green at harvest and will stay that color throughout. Place them on the Bar-B-Que grill for better flavor.

For a smokier flavor try roasting the peppers, remove the charred skin and cut before adding to the soup. You can also roast the corn on the cob. Wet the husk with cool water, wrap in foil and bake or broil on the grill for 35-40 minutes. Unwrap, allow to cool and you will be amazed at how easy the husk comes off.

Minestrone Soup

This Italian specialty can be served as an appetizer or as the main course.

3 qts.	Distilled or Pure Water
1/2 cup	Dry Organic Kidney Beans If using canned, add later in the recipe.
1/2 cup	Dry Garbanzo Beans (Chick Peas) If using canned, add later in the recipe
2 each	Bay Leaves
2 tb.	Minced Garlic
1 each	Large Yellow Onion, diced 1/2"
2 each	Carrots, diced 1/2 inch
2 stalks	Celery, diced 1/2 inch
1 each	Red Pepper, diced 1/2"
1 each	Yellow or Orange Pepper, diced 1/2"
3 each	Vine Ripe Tomatoes, diced 1/2 inch
	(Muir Glen diced tomatoes are also fine)
1 tb.	Oregano Leaves (Fresh herbs are always preferred)
2 tb.	Fresh Basil, chopped
2 tb.	Italian Parsley, chopped, optional
1/8 ts.	Cayenne Pepper
1 tb.	Sea Salt (Optional)
1 cup	Deboles Macaroni
1 pkg.	Fresh Spinach, rinsed, destemmed and chopped

Directions

1. Soak the beans in scalding water for 1-2 hours. Bring distilled water to a boil. Strain the beans, add to the boiling water and cook for 1 hour.
2. Add the next 7 items and simmer for 1 hour.
3. Add the next 6 ingredients and cook until beans are tender.
4. Adjust seasonings as preferred, and add the macaroni and cook about 8 -10 minutes.
 (*At this point you may need to add a little water or vegetable stock if the soup is too thick*)
5. About 5 minutes before serving, add the fresh chopped spinach. Simmer covered for 5 minutes and serve.

Serves 6 - 8

If you are using cooked beans, proceed to Step 2, increase both beans to 1 cup of each.
Add the cooked beans in Step 3 and proceed.

Miso Soup

Miso is the world's first condiment. It is somewhat salty, with a peanut butter like texture. Miso comes in many varieties. You can find light or dark barley miso, red soy bean, garbanzo bean, and miso of many other colors and flavors. Miso is a living food, therefore you need to add it to your hot broth and serve within a few minutes in order to benefit from its stomach soothing abilities.

1 1/4 qts.	Pure or Distilled Water
4 oz.	Domestic Mushrooms, sliced 1/4 inch or Shitake Mushrooms
2 ts.	Minced Garlic
3 tb.	Dark Barley Miso, you can also experiment with other misos
1 each	Carrot, julienne 1/8 X 1 inch strips
3 each	Scallions, sliced 1/4 inch slices
1 ts.	Sesame Oil

Directions

1. Bring the water to a boil in a 2 quart or larger pot.
2. Add the mushrooms and garlic and simmer until mushrooms are tender.
3. Remove about 1/2 cup of the broth into a small bowl and whisk in the miso.
4. Add the carrots, scallions and sesame oil to the soup and continue to simmer.
5. When the miso is dissolved, fold into the soup, adjust seasonings as desired, and turn off the heat. To reheat, do not bring the soup to a boil.

Serves 4 - 6

For a more nutritious and flavorful change, try adding 1/4 cup of wakame (seaweed) slices to the broth at the same time as the mushrooms and proceed with the recipe.

Mushroom Barley Soup

This classic soup actually tastes better since beef brisket has been excluded.

3 qts.	Distilled or Pure Water
1 each	Large Yellow Onion, diced 1/2 inch
2 each	Organic Carrots, 1/2 inch dice
2 each	Celery Stalks, 1/2 inch dice
1 each	Large Bay Leaf
1 cup	Organic Barley
1 lb.	Fresh Mushrooms, sliced 1/4 inch thick
1 tb.	Minced Garlic
3 tb.	Dr. Jensen's Vegetable Base, Bragg Liquid Aminos or Low-Sodium Tamari
1 ts.	Sea Salt (Optional)
1 bunch	Fresh Basil, coarsely chopped
1/8 ts.	Cayenne Pepper

Directions

1. In a large pot bring the water to a boil and add the next 5 ingredients.
2. Simmer for 10 minutes. Add half of the mushrooms and cook for about 30 minutes.
3. Add remaining ingredients and simmer for about 10 minutes. At this point the barley should be fully expanded. You may need to adjust seasonings and vegetable broth if the soup is too thick in texture.

Serves 4 - 6

Navy Bean Soup
(White Bean Soup)

Although this soup has always been known as Navy Bean Soup, you may use Great Northern Beans or lima beans in place of the navy beans.

2 1/2 qts.	Distilled or Pure Water
1 lb.	Organic Navy Beans or any of your favorite White Beans
2 each	Bay Leaves
2 tb.	Minced Garlic
1 each	Large Yellow Onion, diced 1/2"
1 each	Yellow or Orange Pepper, diced 1/2"
2 each	Carrots, peeled if not organic and diced 1/4 inch
12 oz. can	Organic diced Tomatoes (Optional)
2 tb.	Fresh chopped Basil
1/8 ts.	Cayenne Pepper
1 tb.	Sea Salt (Optional)

Directions

1. Soak beans in scalding water for 1-2 hours. Bring distilled water to a boil.
2. Drain the beans and add to boiling water with the bay leaves. Cook for 1 hour skimming the foam from the top.
3. Add all remaining ingredients and cook for about 1 hour or until the beans are tender.
4. Adjust seasonings as needed and garnish with chopped parsley.
5. For a creamier texture remove bay leaf, place soup in blender, cover tightly and puree.

Serves 4 - 6

Black and White Bean Soup

This yin and yang presentation is very easy to do. Puree the two soups separately in a blender. Place a soup bowl between the 2 pots of soup, and with the same size ladle in each hand fill with the soups and ladle into the bowl at the same time.

Potassium Broth
(Vegetable Stock)

This broth is a natural diuretic that can be used as a beverage or a soup base.

1 1/2 gallons	Distilled or Pure Water
3 each	Large Yellow Onions, peeled and qurtered
1 each	Small head Green Cabbage
1 bunch	Celery with leaves, discard core and wash thoroughly
1 lb.	Whole Carrots, organic if possible, scrub well
2 lbs.	Well scrubbed potatoes, (White, Red Potatoes)
1 each	Bouquet Garni (Fresh Thyme, Rosemary, Oregano, Basil, Peppercorns, Garlic Clove and Bay Leaf) Optional for added flavor

Directions

1. Add all ingredients to a large pot and simmer for 2 hours or more.
    You may leave this stock on the stove on low heat for the better part of your day.
2. When finished discard the vegetables and strain the stock.

(The stock will hold well refrigerated for 3-5 days. You may also freeze it for future uses.)

Yields approximately 1 gallon

Cream of Potato & Leek Soup

This soup is great on a chilly day and is excellent served chilled as
"Vichyssoise".

2 qts.	Distilled or Pure Water
2 each	Medium Vidalia or Yellow Onion, peeled, cut in quarters
8 each	Large Red Potatoes, scrubbed and quartered, leave skin on
2 tb.	Minced Garlic
2 ts.	Sea Salt
1/8 ts.	Cayenne Pepper
2 cups	Rice Dream or Soy Milk, scalded
2 each	Leeks, remove tips, split lengthwise and slice in 1/8 inch slices and rinse to remove soil

Directions

1. Bring water to a boil and add the first 5 ingredients.
2. Cook until the potatoes are tender, skimming foam off the top as needed.
3. Remove the pot from the stove and puree the vegetables and broth in a blender and return to the pot.
4. Reduce heat to low, fold in the Rice Dream and leeks and simmer for 10 minutes.
5. Adjust seasonings as desired and serve hot or cold.

Serves 6 - 8

Spring Vegetable Soup

Asparagus is now available year round, so this soup is no longer just meant for the spring.

2 qts	Distilled or Pure Water
12 oz.can	Muir Glen Organic diced Tomatoes
1 each	Large Yellow Onion, diced 1/2 inch
2 each	Organic Carrots, 1/2 inch dice
2 each	Celery Stalks, 1/2 inch dice
2 each	Large Bay Leaf
2 tb.	Minced Garlic
1 tb.	Sea Salt (Optional)
1 each	Zucchini, cut into 1 inch cubes
1 each	Yellow Squash, cut into 1 inch cubes
1 bunch	Fresh Asparagus, sliced in 1 inch pieces
1 bunch	Fresh Basil, coarsely chopped
1/8 ts.	Cayenne Pepper

Directions

1. In a large pot bring the water to a boil and add the next 7 ingredients.
2. Simmer vegetables for 20 minutes, until the carrots are tender.
3. Add the zucchini and squash and cook for 15 minutes.
4. Add the asparagus, basil and cayenne, cover and simmer 5 minutes.
5. Season to taste and serve as soon as the asparagus is tender.

Serves 6 - 8

Curried Cream of Zucchini Soup

As the title denotes, this curry soup has a little zip to it.
Serving over brown rice will turn it into a hearty low-fat stew.

1 1/2 qts.	Distilled or Pure Water
2 each	Medium Vidalia or Yellow Onion, peeled, cut in quarters
2 each	Idaho Potatoes, peeled and cut into 2 inch slices
1 ts.	Ground Coriander
2 tb.	Ground Curry Powder
1 tb.	Minced Garlic
2 ts.	Sea Salt (Optional)
dash	Cayenne Pepper
2 each	Zucchini, cleaned and cut into 1 inch chunks
2 cups	Rice Dream or Soy Milk
1 qt.	Cooked Brown Rice, optional

Directions

1. Bring water to a boil and add the first 7 ingredients.
2. Cook 15 minutes until the potatoes are tender. Add the zucchini and cook until the squash is tender. Do not overcook the zucchini or it will lose some of its bright green color.
3. Remove from stove, puree the vegetable mix in a blender and return to the pot.
4. Reduce heat to low, fold in the Rice Dream until desired thickness is attained.
5. Adjust seasonings and serve hot or cold.

Serves 6 - 8

Split Pea Soup

This is an easy soup to prepare, with a fresh distinctive flavor.

3 qts.	Distilled or Pure Water
1 lb.	Organic Split Peas
1 each	Large Vidalia or Yellow Onion, diced 1/2 inch
2 each	Carrots, diced
3 each	Celery, diced
2 each	Bay Leaves
1 tb.	Sea Salt (Optional)
1/4 ts.	Cayenne Pepper

Directions

1. In a large pot bring the water to a boil. Rinse peas in a strainer, check for stones.
2. Add peas to the pot, cover and simmer for about 30 minutes while stirring occasionally.
3. Skim the foam off the top and add the vegetables and spices.
4. Continue to cook for about 1 hour, skimming the foam as needed, and stirring often to avoid scorching the bottom of the pot.
5. When peas are mushy and the soup has thickened as a result, adjust spices and serve.

Serves up to 8

Garnish with Whole Wheat Pita Croutons or Tofu Hot Dogs or serve with brown rice for a more complete protein.

Salad Dressings

Many of the salad dressings in this chapter are fat-free, others have been emulsified with tofu, tahini or olive oil and have less than 1 gram of saturated fat per serving.

Apple Mustard Dressing

This fat-free dressing is so simple yet so full of flavor.

3 each	Red or Yellow Apples, rinsed, cored and cut into wedges
1/3 cup	Stone Ground Mustard (Low-Sodium) by Westbrae
1/3 cup	Brown Rice Syrup
1/4 cup	Fresh Lemon Juice

Directions
Combine all ingredients in a blender and puree thoroughly.

Yield 24 ounces

For best quality use within 5 days.

• •

Avocado Cucumber Dressing

This dressing goes well on spinach and other leafy greens.
It is also a nice vegetable dip.

2 each	Ripe Avocados, peeled, seeded and quartered
1 each	Medium Red Onion, peeled , cored and quartered
1 each	Large Cucumber, peeled, seeded and quartered
2/3 cup	Distilled Water
1/4 cup	Fresh Lemon Juice
2 ts.	Fresh Minced Garlic
2 tb.	Bragg Liquid Aminos
1/8 ts.	Cayenne Pepper

Directions
Combine all ingredients in a blender and puree thoroughly.
Add more water if a thinner consistency is desired.
You may need to adjust spices to suit your taste.

Yield 32 ounces

For best quality use within 3 days.

Balsamic Vinaigrette

One of our most requested dressings.
The older the Balsamic, the richer the flavor will be.

1 each	Red Apple, quartered, remove seeds
1 each	Vine Ripe Tomato, cored and quartered
1 each	Small Red Onion, peeled and quartered
1 each	Small Avocado, scooped from shell (optional)
2 cups	Distilled or Pure Water
1/2 bunch	Fresh Basil Leaves
1 tb.	Fresh Oregano Leaves
1 ts.	Thyme Leaves (fresh herbs are superior in flavor, if available)
1 tb.	Fresh Minced Garlic
1/3 cup	Balsamic Vinegar
1/4 cup	Fresh Lemon Juice, about 3 lemons
2 tb.	Stoneground Mustard, Westbrae Low-Sodium
dash	Cayenne Pepper
1/4 cup	Cold Pressed Virgin Olive Oil (optional)

Directions

1. Place all ingredients in blender and puree thoroughly.
2. Adjust water and spices to satisfy your taste and consistency.

Yield approximately 1 quart

Dressing should hold for 5 -7 days refrigerated.

Citrus Poppyseed Dressing

This low-sodium dressing goes especially well with a Spinach or Red Leaf Lettuce Salad.

1 cup	Fresh Squeezed Orange Juice
1/2 cup	Lime Juice
1/4 cup	Balsamic Vinegar
1 tb.	Stone Ground Mustard
1/2 cup	Brown Rice Syrup
dash	Cayenne Pepper
1/2 lb.	Extra Firm Silken Tofu, low-fat, wipe dry, cut into cubes
1 tb.	Poppyseeds

Directions

1. Add all ingredients to blender and puree.

Yield approximately 24 ounces

Dressing will keep well for up to 7 days under refrigeration.

Cucumber Dill Dressing

This flavorful dressing can also be served as a cold soup.

2 each	Cucumbers, peeled, seeded and 1/2 inch diced
1 ts.	Minced Garlic
1/4 cup	Fresh Lemon Juice
1/3 cup	Rice Dream or Soy Milk
1 tb.	Bragg Liquid Aminos
2 ts.	Fresh Dill, chopped
dash	Cayenne Pepper
5 oz.	Firm Silken Tofu low-fat, wipe dry, cut into cubes

Directions

1. In a blender combine and puree one of the diced cucumbers and the next 6 ingredients.
2. Slowly add the tofu through the top of the blender while it is running until the desired thickness is attained.
3. Remove the mixture from the blender into a mixing bowl. Fold in the remaining cucumber and adjust seasonings to suit your taste.

Yield approximately 32 ounces

Dressing will hold well for 3 - 5 days refrigerated.

Creamy French Dressing

If there is a healthier French dressing recipe than this one, I could not find it.

1 cup	Fresh Carrot Juice, from a Juicer
1/4 cup	Organic Olive Oil, Cold Pressed, Extra Virgin Oil
4 oz.	Stone Ground Mustard, Low-Sodium
2 tb.	Fresh Squeezed Lemon Juice, about 2 Lemons are needed
1 ts.	Fresh Minced Garlic
Dash	Cayenne Pepper

Directions

Combine all ingredients in a blender and puree thoroughly.

Yield is about 2 cups

For best quality use within 5 days.

• •

Creamy Garlic Dressing

This dressing has many uses. It can add flavor to baked potatoes, steamed vegetables and salads.

1 cup	Rice Dream
10 oz.	Firm Silken Tofu low-fat, wipe dry and cubed
1/4 cup	Fresh Lemon or Lime Jice
1 tb.	Minced Garlic
2 tb.	Bragg Liquid Aminos
2 tb.	Fresh chopped herbs, Basil, Tarragon, or Dill, Optional
dash	Cayenne Pepper or 1/2 ts. Black Pepper

Directions

Combine all ingredients in a blender and puree thoroughly.

Yield approximately 2 1/2 cups.

For best quality use within 5 days .

Guacamole Dip

There is not a faster, more delicious way to prepare this California favorite.

3 each   Ripe Avocados, peel and remove the seed
2 tb.   Fresh Lemon Juice, about 2 lemons
2/3 cup   Mexican Salsa, see recipe on page 195 or use your
              favorite brand
1/4 ts.   Sea Salt (Optional)

Directions

1.   In a non reactive bowl mash the avocados and lemon juice
      together.
2.   Fold in the salsa and adjust seasonings if necessary.
3.   Return the seed of the avocado to the dip to maintain the color
      of avocado.

*For an even faster creamier Guacamole, place all ingredients in a
blender and puree.*

Yield is approximately 2 1/2 cups

Fat-Free Italian Dressing

The vegetables act as the emulsifier of this dressing,
therefore no olive oil is needed.

1 each	Small Red Onion, peeled, cored and quartered
1 each	Large Red Pepper, seeded and quartered
1 each	Large Yellow or Orange Pepper, seeded and quartered
1/2 cup	Apple Cider Vinegar or Brown Rice Vinegar
1/3 cup	Brown Rice Syrup
1/2 cup	Distilled or Pure Water, as needed to obtain desired consistency
1 tb.	Fresh Oregano, chopped
1 tb.	Minced Garlic
dash	Cayenne Pepper

Directions

1. Puree all ingredients together in a blender at high speed for about one minute. Add water if a thinner dressing is desired.

Yield approximately 32 ounces

This dressing will hold well for up to 5 days. Blend well before reusing.

Creamy Italian Dressing

This dressing was created by Yolanda Orient,
our salad dressing expert in the kitchen !

1 each	Medium Red Onion, peeled, cored and quartered
1 each	Red Pepper, seeded and quartered
1 each	Yellow Pepper, seeded and quartered
1/3 cup	Fresh Lemon Juice
2 each	Vine Ripe Tomatoes, quartered
1 each	Avocado, seeded and scoop out the pulp with a spoon
2/3 cup	Distilled Water, as needed to obtain desired consistency
1 tb.	Fresh Oregano, coarsely chopped
1 tb.	Minced Garlic
dash	Cayenne Pepper
1/4 ts.	Sea Salt

Directions

1. Puree all ingredients together in a blender at high speed for about one minute.

Yield approximately 32 ounces

This dressing will hold well for 3 - 5 days. Shake or blend well before reusing.

Lemon Mustard Dressing

This spicy dressing will spruce up any type of salad.
It is also an excellent marinade for Tofu Steaks.

10 oz.	Firm Silken Tofu, Low-Fat
1/4 cup	Distilled or Pure Water
1/4 cup	Fresh Lemon Juice
1/4 cup	Brown Rice Vinegar
1/4 cup	Stone Ground Mustard, low sodium
1 tb.	Minced Garlic
2 tb.	Chopped Parsley
1/4 ts.	Sea Salt, optional
dash	Cayenne Pepper
3 each	Scallions, sliced 1/4 inch slices

Directions

1. Place all ingredients except the scallions in a blender and puree thoroughly.
2. Remove from the blender and fold in the scallions.

Yield is 1 1/2 cups

Dressing should hold for 5-7 days refrigerated.

Mango Basil Vinaigrette

For a year-round tropical flavor this dressing will provide,
use only fresh mangoes.

2 each	Ripe Mangoes, peeled and cut into chunks
1/2 cup	Raw Apple Cider Vinegar or Brown Rice Vinegar
1/2 cup	Organic Apple Juice
1/3 cup	Brown Rice Syrup, optional if the mangoes are not sweet enough
2 tb.	Fresh Chopped Basil

Directions

1. Place all ingredients except the basil in a blender and puree thoroughly.
2. Add the basil to the blender and pulse to incorporate the basil and serve.

Yield is approximately 3 cups

Dressing should hold for 7-10 days refrigerated.

Mexican Vinaigrette

This dressing will certainly enhance a taco salad or any salad for that matter.

3 each	Large Vine Ripe Tomatoes, cored and cut into wedges
1 each	Ripe Avocado, cut in half lengthwise, remove seed and scoop out pulp
1 each	Small Vidalia or Red Onion, peeled and quartered
1 each	Medium Yellow or Orange Pepper, cleaned and quartered
1 each	Small Jalapeno Pepper, seeded and coarsely chopped
2 tb.	Fresh Lemon Juice
1 tb.	Apple Cider or Balsamic Vinegar
1/2 bunch	Cilantro, rinsed and destemmed
2 ts.	Minced Garlic
1/2 ts.	Sea Salt, Optional

Directions

Combine all ingredients in a blender and puree thoroughly, chill before serving.

Yield 1 1/2 qts.

For best quality use within 3 days .

• •

Mexican Vinaigrette Dressing II

This tasty dressing was created as a result of leftovers from a New Year's Eve Party .

2 cups	Mexican Salsa
1/2 cup	Guacamole Dip

Directions

Combine ingredients in blender and puree until smooth.

Yield is 2 1/2 cups

Dressing will hold for 2 - 3 days under refrigeration.

Miso Dressing

For different flavor sensations, you may try other flavored misos.

1 cup	Distilled Water
2 each	Vine Ripe Tomatoes, rinsed and quartered
1/3 cup	Fresh Lemon Juice
3 tb.	Red Miso (available in Oriental or natural food stores)
1 bunch	Scallions, sliced into 1/4 inch slices
1/3 cup	Organic Apple Juice
2 ts.	Minced Garlic
1 tb.	Toasted Sesame Oil
1 tb.	Sesame Tahini (Optional)
2 ts.	Fresh Ground Ginger
1/2 ts.	Thai Chili Paste

Directions

1. Combine all ingredients in the blender, but first set aside half of the sliced scallions.
2. Remove from blender and fold in the remaining scallions for garnish.

Yield approximately 28 ounces

Dressing will keep well for 5 days refrigerated. Shake well before using.

Mustard Tahini Dressing

This is the hands-down favorite dressing of our guests.
It has such a tantalizing array of taste sensations.

2/3 cup	Water, use as necessary to obtain desired consistency
1/2 cup	Fresh Lemon Juice
1/2 cup	Sesame Tahini
1/3 cup	Brown Rice Syrup
1/4 cup	Stone Ground Mustard by Westbrae, low sodium
2 tb.	Bragg Liquid Aminos
2 ts.	Minced Garlic
2 tb.	Fresh Chopped Italian Parsley
dash	Cayenne Pepper

Directions

1. In a blender combine all ingredients.
2. Add additonal water slowly for a thinner consistency.

Yield 20 ounces

This dressing will hold well for up to one week. It may need to be thinned
with a little cool water upon reusing.

Oriental Vinaigrette

This dressing serves as a marinade for Seaweed Cole Slaw, Chinese vegetable salad, grilled tofu steaks or as a salad dressing.

1 cup	Pure or Distilled Water
1/2 cup	Low Sodium Tamari or Shoyu
1/2 cup	Brown Rice Syrup
1/3 cup	Rice Vinegar, or Cider Vinegar is OK in a pinch
1 each	Vine Ripe Tomato, quartered (Optional)
2 tb.	Toasted Sesame Seeds, cook in saute pan on high heat
1 tb.	Minced Garlic
1 ts.	Thai Chili Paste
1 ts.	Toasted Sesame Oil

Directions

1. Place all ingredients in blender and puree thoroughly.
2. Adjust water and spices to satisfy your taste and consistency.

Yield approximately 2 1/2 cups

Dressing should hold for 7 days or more refrigerated.

Pineapple Mustard Dressing

This dressing gives a special flavor to a spinach or leafy salad .

1 cup	Organic Apple Juice
1 cup	Fresh Squeezed Orange Juice
1 cup	Fresh cut Pineapple chunks
2 tb.	Stone Ground Mustard (Low-Sodium)
1/2 each	Ripe Avocado, peeled and seeded
1 ts.	Minced Garlic

Directions

Combine all ingredients in a blender and puree thoroughly.

Yield 28 ounces

For best quality use within 5-7 days.

• •

Ranch Dressing

This dressing is also a nice party dip for dry snacks or vegetable trays.

8 oz.	Firm Silken Tofu low-fat, wipe dry and cubed
2 each	Scallions, chopped
1/4 cup	Nayonnaise or Soy Yogurt, available in natural food stores
1/4 cup	Distilled Water
2 tb.	Fresh Squeezed Lemon Juice
2 ts.	Fresh Minced Garlic
Dash	Cayenne Pepper
1 tb.	Fresh Chopped Dill
1 ts.	Ground Cumin
1 tb.	Bragg Liquid Aminos

Directions

Combine all ingredients in a blender and puree thoroughly.

Yield approximately 2 1/2 cups

For best quality use within 5 days.

Raspberry Vinaigrette

The raspberries serve as a wonderful emulsifier for this fat-free dressing.

1/2 cup	Raw Apple Cider Vinegar or Brown Rice Vinegar
1/2 bunch	Fresh Basil, chopped
1 pt.	Raspberries, sorted and rinsed
1/2 cup	Brown Rice Syrup

Directions

1. Puree all ingredients in blender.
2. If the raspberries are too sour, add more Brown Rice Syrup to sweeten.

Yield approximately 20 ounces

Dressing will hold well for 5 - 7 days under refrigeration.

Russian Dressing

Most Russian dressings use corn syrup as the sweetner.
This version is much lower in sugar content.

1 each	Large Vine Ripe Tomato, cored and quartered
2/3 cup	Organic Tomato Puree
1/2 cup	Distilled Water
1/2 cup	Brown Rice Syrup
5 oz.	Firm Silken Tofu low-fat, drained and cut into cubes
2 tb.	Raw Apple Cider Vinegar or Brown Rice Vinegar
1 tb.	Stone Ground Mustard
2 tb.	Minced Red Onion or 1 tb. Onion Powder
1/4 ts.	Sea Salt (Optional)
Dash	Cayenne Pepper

Directions

Combine all ingredients in a blender and puree thoroughly.
You may need to add more water if the dressing is too thick.

Yield approximately 32 ounces

For best quality use within 5 days.

Sundried Tomato Vinaigrette

This dressing is wonderful on a salad or on your favorite hot or cold pasta.

1 cup	Distilled or Pure Water, heated
1/2 cup	Sundried Tomatoes, chopped coarse
1/3 cup	Apple Cider Vinegar or Balsamic Vinegar
1 bunch	Fresh Basil, chopped
2 each	Vine Ripe Tomatoes, quartered
2 ts.	Minced Garlic
1/4 cup	Organic Olive Oil (Optional)
1/4 ts.	Sea Salt (Optional)
dash	Cayenne Pepper

Directions

1. Soften sundried tomatoes in hot water for 5 minutes. Strain and reserve the liquid.
2. Combine the broth from the soaking tomatoes and all other ingredients in a blender and puree thoroughly.

Yield approximately 32 ounces

This dressing will hold well for 5 days refrigerated.

Tahini Dressing

Adding the basil to this recipe gives it a sweeter, more enjoyable flavor.

2 cups	Distilled or Pure Water
1/2 cup	Fresh Lemon Juice
1/3 cup	Barley Malt or Brown Rice Syrup
2 ts.	Ground Cumin
1 tb.	Minced Garlic
2 tb.	Fresh Chopped Basil (Optional)
1 cup	Sesame Tahini

Directions

1. In a blender combine all ingredients except the tahini.
2. Add the tahini slowly until desired consistency.

CAUTION !

Do not place the tahini in the blender until last. It is very heavy and has been known to burn up a blender motor before its time!

Yield 32 ounces

This dressing will hold well for up to one week. It may need to be thinned with a little cool water upon reusing.

Raspberry Tahini Dressing

My good friend and colleague Chef Ken Hubscher
collaborated on this recipe.

1/2 pt.	Fresh Raspberries, rinsed
1/4 cup	Rice Dream or other rice milk
1/4 cup	Brown Rice Syrup
3 tb.	Sesame Tahini
1 tb.	Low Sodium Tamari
2 tb.	Apple Cider Vinegar or Raspberry Vinegar

Directions

1. Place all ingredients in blender and puree thoroughly. If the raspberries are too sour, add more brown rice syrup.

Yield approximately 1 1/2 cups

Dressing should hold for 5-7 days refrigerated. If too thick, add a little cool water upon reusing until desired consistency is attained.

Tarragon Vinaigrette

This dressing goes particularly well over a baby spinach salad with mushrooms, red onions and pita croutons.

1/3 cup	Raw Apple Cider Vinegar or Rice Vinegar
1/4 cup	Pure or Distilled Water
5 oz.	Firm Silken Tofu, low-fat if available
2 tb.	Stone Ground Mustard
2 tb.	Brown Rice Syrup
2 tb.	Fresh Lemon Juice
1 ts.	Minced Garlic
1/4 ts.	Sea Salt, Optional
1 tb.	Tarragon Leaves

Directions

1. Place all ingredients except the tarragon in a blender and puree thoroughly.
2. Add the tarragon to the blender and pulse to incorporate.

Refrigerate the dressing until chilled. This will enhance the flavor of this dressing.

Yield is approximately 2 cups

Dressing should hold for 5-7 days refrigerated.

Thousand Island Dressing

This is not one of our fat-free dressings, but it is a classic one.

1 each	Small Red Onion, diced
1 each	Medium Red Pepper, diced
1/4 cup	Green Olives, chopped
1 ts.	Minced Garlic
2 tb.	Chopped Italian Parsley
1/4 cup	Brown Rice Syrup
1/2 cup	Soy Yogurt or Nayonnaise
2/3 cup	Organic Tomato Puree
4 oz.	Firm Silken Tofu drained and cut into 1 inch cubes
1/2 cup	Distilled or Pure Water

Directions

1. After preparing the first 6 ingredients, set aside in a bowl.
2. Combine in a blender the brown rice syrup, tomato puree, yogurt, tofu and water.
3. Add the vegetables to the blender and pulse until incorporated.
4. If you prefer a creamier dressing turn the blender to high speed and puree.

Yield approximately 24 ounces

For best quality use within 7 days.

Delicious Soy Yogurt Dressings

These are wonderfully refreshing sauces to go with your favorite tropical fruits. They can be used as an accompaniment to a fresh fruit display, or as a replacement for mayonnaise in a Waldorf or other salads.

Orange Honey Yogurt Dressing

1/2 cup	Fresh Orange Juice, about 4 oranges
2 ts.	Orange Zest, obtain from oranges before cutting and squeezing
3/4 cup	Dairyless Soy Yogurt
1/2 cup	Honey

Combine all, ingredients in a mixing bowl with a wire whip until smooth.

Yield 1 3/4 cups

• •

Guava Yogurt Dressing

3/4 cup	Guava Concentrate (in the frozen section Latin Grocery area)
1 1/2 cups	Dairyless Soy Yogurt

Combine all ingredients in a mixing bowl with a wire whip until smooth.

Yield 2 1/4 cups

Passion Fruit Dressing

3/4 cup	Passion Fruit Concentrate (in the frozen section Latin Grocery area)
1 1/2 cup	Dairyless Soy Yogurt

Combine all ingredients in a mixing bowl with a wire whip until smooth.

Yield 2 1/4 cups

• •

Banana Yogurt Dressing

1/2 cup	Soy Yogurt
1/2 cup	Fresh Orange Juice
2 each	Very Ripe Bananas, peeled and cut into 1 inch chunks
1/2 ts.	Ground Cinnamon
1 ts.	Vanilla Extract

Directions

1.   Place all ingredients in blender and puree thoroughly.

Yield approximately 1 3/4 cups

Dressing should hold for 3 days or more refrigerated.

Strawberry Yogurt Dressing

There are only 45 calories in 1 cup of strawberries.
They make a great dressing too.

1 cup	Fresh Strawberries or Raspberries, hulled and cut in half
2/3 cup	Soy Yogurt
1/3 cup	Organic Apple Juice
2 ts.	Fresh chopped Peppermint (Optional)
1/2 ts.	Vanilla Extract

Directions

1. Place all ingredients in blender and puree thoroughly.

Yield approximately 2 cups

Dressing should hold for 3 days or more refrigerated.

Pasta Entrees

Pasta with Pesto Sauce, Wild Mushrooms and
Sundried Tomatoes.

Pasta
Varieties and Cooking Methods

The popularity of pasta has never been greater than today. As a result many of us eat pasta 3 or more times per week. For that reason, I thought it would be helpful to present you with some important information that may help you make the right choices in choosing your pastas.

Our pasta of choice at the spa and also in this book are whole-grain pastas that have not been enriched. There are many brands on the market that are excellent choices. The brand we have experienced most is DeBoles Pastas. They are available in most grocery stores as well as the majority of health food stores. DeBoles pastas have many varieties and come in traditional shapes and sizes. What separates DeBoles from most pastas is that the grain in the pasta, for example whole wheat, and Jerusalem artichokes are the only ingredients. Deboles also has a semolina pasta and for those who have an allergy to wheat gluten they also make a corn pasta with the only other ingredient being Jerusalem artichokes. These are not enriched pastas. Your typical supermarket pastas are enriched pastas. Due to the additional milling and processing of the these pastas, they have been stripped of their fiber and essential B vitamins. When you read the label of these "enriched pastas", you will also see that B vitamins riboflavin, niacin and thiamine needed to be added, as I describe it, to "re-enrich" the pastas. By consuming whole-grain pastas, we are allowing ourselves better nutritional value, added protein and fiber, which results in better digestion of these foods.

There are many other whole-grain pastas available in our local health food stores. Quinoa pasta is wheat-free and comes from the oldest grain known to man. Its bright yellow color when cooked brings a special appearance to a pasta presentation.

Lupinni pasta is made from the lupin bean. Rich in protein, somewhat hearty in flavor, this pasta is unique in the fact that it is not starchy or sticky after the cooking process.

There are other whole-grain pastas to choose from such as amaranth, spelt, and rye. Soba noodles are popular in Oriental cooking and are made of buckwheat flour. Once you have experienced these superior pastas you will never go back to enriched pastas again.

Cooking pasta is rather simple. Let your water come to boil and follow the manufacturer's instructions for the allotted time. Do not cook at a high boiling point or you may cause the pasta to break apart. I no longer add salt or oil to the pasta cooking water, yet we achieve the same results, with additional sodium and fat calories being avoided. If you have made a flavorful sauce to complement the pasta, there is no need to add salt to the cooking water to bring out more flavor in the pasta! Vegetable oil is comprised of 100 percent fat calories and has been known to assist in keeping the pasta from sticking. What I suggest to try is after the pasta has reached your personal tenderness texture, pour into a strainer, and "shock" the pasta with cold running water while stirring gently with a wooden spoon or rubber spatula. This stops the cooking of the pasta, and removes some of the starchiness as well. To reheat the pasta, simply dip the strainer into a pot of boiling water to reheat the pasta, shake off the excess water, toss with your heated sauce and serve. That is how all of your favorite restaurants have been reheating their pasta for your dinner. Why should we do it any differently at home? This also allows you to cook your pasta at an earlier time, and then reheat it when needed. From time to time splash the pasta in the strainer with cool water to avoid any sticking. Do not submerge your pasta in water for any long periods of time. This will affect the palatability and texture.

I hope this information will be of assistance to you in making the right choices in pasta.

Pasta with Pesto Sauce,
Wild Mushrooms and Sundried Tomatoes

This is one of our most requested entrees. Feel free to try other pasta varieties.

12 oz.	Durum Semolina Angel Hair Pasta or other Pasta favorite
1 ts.	Canola Oil
1 tb.	Minced Garlic
2 ts.	Thyme Leaves
1/2 ts.	Sea Salt
4 each	Portabella Mushrooms, destemmed, scrape off gills on the underside with a spoon and slice 1/4 inch

and / or

1/2 lb.	Shitake Mushrooms, destemmed and cut in half
1 cup	Sundried Tomatoes, softened in hot water, then sliced 1/2 inch thick
1/2 cup	Pesto Sauce, recipe on page 202
1/4 cup	Soy Parmesan Cheese

Directions

1. Bring a pot of water to boil and cook the angel hair 4-5 minutes or until al dente.
2. Strain pasta and rinse with cool water and set aside.
3. Heat canola oil, add garlic, mushrooms and spices, cover and cook until tender.
4. Reheat pasta by quickly submerging with a strainer in boiling water and strain.
5. In a bowl add the pasta, mushrooms without the liquid, sundried tomatoes and pesto.
6. Serve hot and top with a soy parmesan cheese and basil sprig garnish.

Serves 3 - 4

"Pad Thai-Style" Noodles with Peanut Sauce

The peanut sauce provides a spicy, protein-rich change from traditional pasta recipes.

2 each	Zucchini, split lengthwise, scoop out seeds in the center with a spoon and slice into 1/2 thick slices
2 each	Carrots, peel and cut into 2 inch by 1/2 inch sticks
3 each	Scallions, sliced in 1/4 inch slices
1 cup	Frozen Baby Peas, thawed
8 oz. box	DeBoles Fettucine or Linguini Semolina Pasta, break in half and cook 6-8 minutes until al dente, place in collander and shock with cool water
1 1/2 cups	Spicy Thai Peanut Sauce, recipe on page 201

Directions

1. While preparing the vegetables, cook the pasta according to instructions and set aside.
2. Steam the vegetables 4-5 minutes until just tender.
3. While the vegetables are steaming begin preparing the peanut sauce in a large pot. If you desire a thinner peanut sauce add more water.
4. Add the pasta and vegetables to the peanut sauce, toss and serve when heated.

Serves 3 - 4

The perfect vegetable to complement this pasta dish is the steamed Broccoli with Garlic, Tamari and Coconut Sauce found on page 159.

Tofu Vegetable Lasagne

The beauty of this recipe besides the lower fat and calories is the tremendous ease of assembly. Be gone with boiling your Lasagne Noodles, then hoping you have enough pieces to make 1 pan. We will use the noodles right from the box.

Tofu Filling

2 lb.	Firm Tofu, pressed, drained, then crumbled or mashed with potato masher
2 tb.	Roasted Sesame Tahini
2 tb.	Yellow Miso
1 head	Broccoli, cut into small florettes, steamed about 3 minutes
1 cup	Julienne or sliced Carrots 1/4 inch
1 each	Zucchini and/or Summer Squash, quartered and 8 oz. Mushrooms, sliced in 1/2 inch slices, Optional
1/2 pkg.	Fresh Spinach, cleaned and stemmed, cut leaves in half
1 bunch	Fresh Basil, chopped coarse

Blend the tahini and miso together with the tofu, combine with remaining ingredients and set aside for future assemly.

Lasagne Assembly Instructions

You will need:

2 qts.	Marinara Sauce, recipe on page 194
1-2 boxes	Whole Wheat or Durum Semolina Lasagne Noodles
1 pkg.	Soy Mozzarella Cheese, fat free, shredded
1 jar	Soy Parmesan Cheese, Lite n Less by Soyco

1. Preheat oven to 400 degrees. You will need a 9 X 13 casserole dish or baking pan that is a minimum of 2 1/2 inches deep.
2. Line the bottom of the pan with marinara sauce.
3. Layer the uncooked noodles, slightly overlapping over the sauce.
4. Spread a little more sauce evenly over the noodles.
5. Place half of the vegetable tofu mix evenly over the noodles, packing firmly.
6. Place 1 more layer of Lasagne noodles over the vegetable tofu mix in same fashion as the first layer. If you need to break the noodles in order to fit them in the pan do so, but remember to overlap them.
7. Pour the marinara sauce evenly over the top layer of noodles.
8. Sprinkle the shredded mozzarella evenly over the the noodles. Cover the pan with plastic wrap, then with foil and bake for about one hour and 15 minutes.
9. Remove casserole from oven, uncover carefully and sprinkle the soy parmesan cheese over the top. Set oven to broil setting at 500 degrees. Return casserole to top rack to brown the cheese. Remove and let cool for about 10 minutes. This will allow the casserole to "setup" and hold together well for serving.
10. After cutting be sure to trim around the edges of casserole before serving.
11. Reheat the remaining marinara sauce and serve with the lasagne.

Serves 6 - 8

Pasta with Wild Mushroom Ragout

Feel free to try this hearty dish with any variety of your favorite mushrooms.

1 tb.	Organic Cold Pressed Olive Oil
1 each	Medium Yellow Onion, diced 1/2"
1 each	Red Pepper, diced 1/2"
1 each	Yellow Pepper, diced 1/2"
1 tb.	Minced Garlic
4 each	Portabella Mushrooms, destemmed, scrape off gills, slice into 1/4 inch slices, or 1 lb. Shitake or other mushrooms
1/8 ts.	Crushed Red Pepper
2 each	Bay Leaf
1 tb.	Oregano Leaves
1 bunch	Fresh Basil, chopped
3/4 cup	Sundried Tomatoes, chopped coarse
4 ea.	Vine Ripe Tomatoes, diced, or 24 oz. Muir Glen Organic Diced Tomatoes
1 can	Muir Glen Organic Tomato Puree or other
12 oz. pkg	Whole Wheat Rotinni or other pasta favorites
2 qts.	Distilled Water or Pure Water

Directions

1. Heat olive oil, add onions, peppers, garlic and saute.
2. Add mushrooms, cayenne and herbs, continue to simmer until tender.
3. Add the tomato products and simmer 30-45 minutes to incorporate all the flavors.
4. Bring water to a boil, add pasta and cook 6-8 minutes, until al dente.
5. Strain pasta, and serve with the mushroom ragout.
6. For an added touch, sprinkle the pasta with soy parmesan cheese.

Serves 4

Penne Pasta Primavera

*You may substitute any of your favorite pastas for the penne in this recipe.
You can also replace the basil olive oil mix with the lower fat marinara or
alfredo sauce recipes.*

1 lb.	Durum Semolina Penne Pasta or other favorite
1 head	Broccoli, cut into florettes
2 each	Carrots, bias sliced 1/4 inch
2 oz.	Snow Peas
1 each	Zucchini or Yellow Squash, halved lengthwise and cut into 1/2 inch slices
2 each	Vine Ripe Tomatoes, cored and cut into wedges
1 bunch	Fresh Basil Leaves
4 oz.	Organic Cold Pressed Olive Oil
2 ts.	Fresh Minced Garlic
1/2 ts.	Sea Salt, optional
dash	Cayenne Pepper
4 oz.	Soy Parmesan Cheese

Directions

1. Add pasta to boiling water and cook 6-8 minutes until tender, stirring occasionally.
2. Remove and strain pasta and rinse with cool water and drain.
3. Bring a second pot of water to a boil in order to blanch the vegetables.
4. Prep all vegetables and cook or steam until just tender. Do not cook the tomatoes.
5. Place olive oil, basil, garlic, and spices in blender and puree.
6. In a large pot heat the pasta, cooked vegetables and tomatoes.
7. When the pasta and vegetables are hot, fold in the basil sauce, soy cheese and serve. Garnish with remaining soy parmesan cheese and fresh basil sprigs .

Serves 6 - 8

*You may also serve this pasta as a cold salad. Feel free to substitute the
vegetables in this recipe with other ones such as wild mushrooms, asparagus,
spinach or whatever is in season.*

Spinach Lasagne
with Grilled Vegetables

If you enjoy using the Bar-B-Que grill, this low-fat lasagne will certainly appeal to you.

1 each	Eggplant, peeled and sliced lengthwise in long 1/2 inch slices
3 each	Zucchini, remove stems, cut lengthwise into long 1/2 inch slices
3 each	Summer Squash, remove stems, cut lengthwise into long 1/2 inch slices
1 each	Large Red Pepper, roasted, skinned and sliced lengthwise into 1/2 inch slices
1/3 cup	Organic Virgin Olive Oil
2 ts.	Minced Garlic
1 each	Small Yellow or Red Pepper, quartered
1 tb.	Oregano Leaves
1/2 ts.	Sea Salt, optional
dash	Cayenne Pepper
1 1/2 qts.	Marinara Sauce, recipe on 194
2 boxes	Spinach Lasagne Noodles, do not cook the noodles
1 pkg.	Soy Mozzarella Cheese, fat free, shredded
1 jar	Soy Parmesan Cheese, Lite n Less by Soyco

1. Prepare the Marinara sauce in advance to make this recipe even easier to assemble.
2. Turn on the grill to high heat setting. Slice the vegetables as described.
3. In a blender puree the olive oil and the next 5 items. Brush oil over the sliced vegetables.
4. Place the vegetables on the grill until dark grill marks appear, then flip over and repeat.

Spinach Lasagne
with Grilled Vegetables *(con't)*
Assembly Instructions

If you would prefer using an oven, preheat oven on the broil setting to 500 degrees. Place the vegetables on a pan, brush with the oil mixture and broil on the top rack until golden. Flip the vegetables over and repeat. Remove and cool the vegetables before proceeding.

5. Set the vegetables aside and roast the red peppers until charred and remove skin.
6. Preheat oven to 400 degrees.
   You will need a 10 x 12 x 2 1/2 inch deep casserole dish.
7. Line the bottom of the casserole with marinara sauce.
8. Layer the uncooked noodles, slightly overlapping on the sauce.
9. Spread the grilled eggplant evenly over the noodles and cover lightly with sauce.
10. Layer the noodles, slightly overlapping over the eggplant, and cover with a little sauce.
11. Layer the zucchini evenly over the noodles and cover with more noodles and sauce.
12. Place the grilled squash evenly over the noodles, and cover lightly with sauce.
13. Sprinkle the soy mozzarella evenly over the squash followed by the red pepper slices.
14. Cover the casserole with plastic wrap, then with foil and bake for 1 hour. Remove casserole and set oven to broil at 500 degrees.
15. Uncover carefully and sprinkle the parmesan cheese over the top and return to bake on the top rack until golden brown. Remove and allow to cool for about 10 minutes.
This will allow the casserole to "setup" and hold together well before cutting.
16. After cutting be sure to trim around the edges of casserole before serving.
   Reheat the remaining marinara sauce and serve with the lasagne.

Serves 6 - 8

Baked Ziti
with Meatless Marinara Sauce

It is very easy to duplicate this old favorite by using a textured vegetable protein meat substitute, made by Morningstar, Gimme Lean, or use crumbled Boca Burgers.

Meatless Marinara Sauce

2 ts.	Cold Pressed Virgin Olive Oil or 1/2 cup Vegetable Broth
2 each	Yellow Onion, diced 1/2 inch
1 each	Red Pepper, diced
1 each	Yellow Pepper, diced
1 tb.	Minced Garlic
1 1/2 lb.	Meat Substitute, crumble before cooking
12 oz. can	Muir Glen Organic Diced Tomatoes, or fresh diced tomatoes
12 oz. can	Muir Glen Organic Tomato Puree
2 tb.	Oregano Flakes, fresh chopped is preferred
2 tb.	Fresh Chopped Basil Leaves
2 each	Bay Leaf
1/2 ts.	Cayenne Pepper
1/2 ts.	Sea Salt

Directions

1. Heat a large pot and saute the oil, onions, garlic and peppers. Cook until vegetables are tender.
2. Place the meat substitute with the vegetables and continue to cook, stirring occasionally.
3. Add the remaining ingredients, cover and simmer for about 1 hour. Adjust seasoning to suit your personal tastes.

Yield is about 2 quarts

Baked Ziti *(continued)*

Casserole Assembly

1 lb.	Deboles Brand Ziti, cook until just tender and drain
2 qts.	Meatless Marinara Sauce
8 oz.	Fat Free Soy Mozzarella Cheese

Directions

1. Preheat oven to 400 degrees.
2. While the ziti and meat sauce are cooking, shred the soy mozzarella.
3. In a large mixing bowl fold together the meat sauce and ziti.
4. Place the pasta in a large casserole dish and top with the shredded cheese.
5. Bake until the cheese is slightly brown and serve.

Serves 6 - 8

*You may also try replacing the meat substitute
with broccoli and mushrooms for variety.*

Portabella Mushrooms Parmesan with Garlic Pasta

If you have missed old favorites like Chicken or Veal Parmesan, I think this recipe will provide you with a healthier alternative. We will "oven-fry" the mushrooms and use fat-free soy mozzarella cheese to reduce the saturated fat calories.

4 each	Large Portabella Mushrooms, remove stem, scoop out the gills on the underside and rinse with cool water
2 cups	Whole Wheat Bread Crumbs
2 tb.	Oregano Flakes
1 cup	Water
1/3 cup	Egg Replacer, found in natural food stores
2/3 cup	Whole-Grain Flour
1/4 cup	Canola Oil
1 quart	Marinara Sauce, recipe on page 194
6 oz.	Fat-Free Soy Mozzarella Cheese
2 tb.	Soy Parmesan Cheese, Lite n Less
8 oz.	Durum Semolina Pasta or other unrefined pasta, cooked al dente
1/2 cup	Cilantro Aioli Sauce, recipe on page 189,
	replace the cilantro with fresh basil for this recipe

Directions

1. While cleaning the mushrooms, preheat the oven to 400 degrees.
2. To bread the mushrooms: place in one bowl the whole-grain flour.
   In a second bowl combine the egg replacer and the water.
   In the third bowl mix the bread crumbs and oregano.
   Dust the mushrooms on both sides in the flour. Then dip the mushrooms in the egg replacer mixture. Lastly, coat the mushrooms with the bread crumbs.
3. Oil a sheet pan generously with the canola oil.
4. Place the breaded mushrooms with the cap side facing down on the sheet pan.
5. When all the mushrooms have been placed on the pan, bake on the bottom rack of the oven about 20 minutes or until the bottom is brown.
6. Remove mushrooms from the oven and flip over with a metal spatula.
7. Return to the oven and bake 12-15 minutes until both sides are crispy.
8. Heat the marinara sauce and place about one cup in the bottom of a casserole.
9. Ladle a little of the marinara over the top of the mushrooms.
10. Cover the mushrooms with the cheeses and bake on the top oven rack for 12-15 minutes or until the cheese is melted and lightly browned.
11. Heat the cooked pasta or other grains with the aioli sauce, place one mushroom partially over the pasta and serve with the remaining marinara.

Serves 4

Homemade Pasta

3 1/3 cups	Whole Wheat Flour
1 cup	Full-Fat Soy Flour
1 ts.	Sea Salt
2/3 cup	Distilled Water

(For flavored pasta use 1/3 cup water and 1/3 cup cooked vegetable puree.)
Spinach, red beets and carrots are the most popular flavors and colors!

Directions

1. In a large bowl, mix together the flours and sea salt.
2. Pour in the water and vegetable puree and mix with a strong fork until a ball forms.
3. Dust a clean dry table with flour and knead the dough for about 10 minutes.
4. Cover dough completely with plastic and let rest for 15 minutes.
5. Cut the dough into 4 equal pieces and roll out to 1/16 inch, on a floured surface.
   (*Be sure to keep the remaining dough covered until you are ready to use it.)*
6. It is normal for the dough to stick to the surface at times. Sprinkle on some flour to prevent sticking.

To make the dough in a food processor, add flours and salt. With the motor running, add the water and vegetable mix and process about 30 seconds until a ball forms. Be sure to check the manufacturer's instructions as well. You may also use an electric mixer with a dough hook to achieve the same results.

7. Hang the rolled dough to dry on a pasta rack, or an upright dish rack before cutting.
8. After about 10 minutes of drying, place the dough back onto a lightly floured table, loosely roll the dough like a jelly roll and slice the dough into your favorite widths, be it linguini, fettucini or lasagne noodle. Flour cut noodles lightly and form gently into little nests until ready to cook.

If you have a manual or electric pasta machine, cut the dough into 4 pieces, lightly flour and run through as you normally would.

9. Bring a pot of water to a rolling boil, add the pasta, continue to boil but not too rapidly, about 6 minutes. Be sure to stir the pasta occasionally to prevent clumping.
10. Place the cooked pasta in a strainer and "shock" with cool running water momentarily.
11. To reheat the pasta, you can simmer it with your favorite sauce, or dip it quickly into a pot of boiling water to bring it back up in temperature, strain it and fold in a pesto or other sauce.

Serves 3 - 4

Sicilian Style Orzo

Orzo is a rice-shaped pasta that cooks in 6-8 minutes. It is popular in the Greek cuisine and a nice change from traditional pasta.

3 qts.	Distilled or Pure Water
1 lb.	Whole Wheat or Tricolored Orzo, or other pasta favorite
1 lb.	Domestic Mushrooms, cut in half
1 bunch	Fresh Basil Leaves
1 tb.	Minced Garlic
1/2 cup	Organic Cold Pressed Olive Oil
1/2 ts.	Sea Salt, optional
dash	Cayenne Pepper
1 cup	Sundried Tomatoes, softened and cut into 1/2 inch slices
1/3 cup	Black Olives, sliced
1/3 cup	Green Olives with Pimientos, sliced
1/4 cup	Capers (Optional)
1/3 cup	Grated Soy Parmesan Cheese

Directions

1. Bring water to a rolling boil, add pasta and stir frequently. Cook 6-8 minutes, or until just tender. Steam mushrooms and set aside.
2. Strain pasta in a colander and rinse quickly with cool water and strain. To reheat orzo, pour scalding water over and strain well.
3. Combine next 5 ingredients in a blender for a superior consistency and flavor.
4. In a large pan heat the pasta with the dressing and add the remaining ingredients and serve.
5. Garnish with soy parmesan cheese and a basil sprig.

Serves 4 - 6

This dish can also be served as a cold salad.

Soba or Lo Mein Style Noodles

Try this pasta for an Oriental theme-dinner with Stir-Steamed Vegetables.

2 qts.	Distilled Water
12 oz.	Buckwheat Soba Noodles or Durum Semolina Linguini for Lo Mein Style Noodles
1 bunch	Scallions, sliced 1/4" thick
2 ts.	Minced Garlic
1/4 cup	Low-Sodium Tamari or Soy Sauce
2 tb.	Water
1 ts.	Toasted Sesame Oil
1 tb.	Toasted Sesame Seeds (Optional)

Directions

1. Bring water to a boil, cook noodles 6 - 8 minutes until tender, rinse with cool water and strain.
2. Have another pot of hot water on the stove to reheat the noodles at service time.
3. In separate saute pan heat tamari, water, garlic and scallions.
4. Submerge the Soba Noodles in the scalding water to reheat and strain again .
5. Add the noodles to the saute pan, toss with the sesame oil and sesame seeds and serve.

Serves 3 - 4

For variety try adding water chestnuts and julienne carrots to the pasta.

Introduction to Tofu

Tofu is made by curdling the soy milk which is extracted from cooked soybeans. Due to its neutral flavor and ability to take on the whatever flavor you decide to use as a marinade or sauce, tofu is one of the ideal entrees in the Vegetarian Cuisine! Its versatility allows tofu to be used in salads, entrees and desserts. If you freeze tofu, then thaw and press dry, it has a meat-like texture and can be used in casseroles.

There are 2 types of tofu available, regular or silken. Regular tofu comes in extra firm, firm and soft. For tofu steaks and stir-fry, regular extra firm or firm tofu is recommended. Silken tofu comes in soft, firm and extra firm, and its custard-like texture make it superb for dressings, desserts and sauces.

There are approximately 120 calories in a 4 ounce serving of tofu. There are 6 grams of fat per 4 ounce serving, however less than 1/2 gram of the fat is saturated fat! Tofu is protein-rich, low in sodium, and a good source of iron, calcium, potassium and Vitamins B and E.

When you purchase regular tofu packed in water, you first need to drain the tofu. We will then wrap the tofu in paper towels to remove the outer moisture. However, tofu is porous and the center of the loaf remains very moist. Unwrap the tofu and place in a collander with a bowl beneath the collander for the drippings. Now place another bowl or pan on top of the tofu with another heavy object like a melon or a book to weigh down the tofu. Allow to press the tofu about 1 hour. At this point you can cut the tofu into steaks for grilling, into cubes for a stir-fry, crumble or mash for lasagne, stuffed shells or scrambled tofu, or add in blender to create emulsified salad dressings! If you do not use all the tofu at once, submerge in water and refrigerate. Change the water every other day and the tofu should store well for 7-10 days.

Silken tofu only needs to be removed from its package, wipe dry lightly and proceed to prepare as needed in salad dressings or in hot or cold sauces. It does not need to be kept refrigerated until it is opened. There are low-fat varieties available as well. The question has been asked, "What about the tofu in open liquid in the Oriental stores?" If the environment is sanitary and the temperature is maintained below 40 degrees, out of the danger zone, which is temperature between 41-140 degrees, then you can purchase with peace of mind. Otherwise, a safe bet is the tofu that is sealed and stored refrigerated in the dairy section of most health food stores.

There are numerous tofu recipes throughout the book from enchiladas to whipped cream. I am sure you will find many favorites and will become a tofu aficionado in a very short time!

98

Tofu Entrees

Clockwise from top, Grilled Tofu Steaks,
Scrambled Tofu, and delicious Tofu Meatballs.

Scrambled Tofu

This is our healthy version of Scrambled Eggs.
Great for a fast breakfast, or a hot protein dish for any meal.

1 lb.	Extra Firm Tofu, drained, pressed dry and crumbled or mashed
1/4 cup	Vegetable Broth or Distilled Water
1 each	Small Yellow Onion, diced 1/2 inch or
4 each	Scallions, cleaned and cut into 1/2 inch slices
1 each	Small Red Pepper, diced 1/2 inch
1 cup	Sliced Mushrooms, optional
1 ts.	Minced Garlic
2 ts.	Curry Powder or 1 ts. Tumeric for color if the curry is too spicy for you
1 tb.	Bragg Liquid Aminos or 1 ts. Low-Sodium Tamari

Directions

1. Heat saute pan and add vegetable broth to scald.
2. Add vegetables and cook until tender. (If you prefer browned vegetables, replace the water with 1 ts. canola oil and saute on medium high heat)
3. Add the tofu and seasonings, cook until hot, drain excess liquid and serve.

Serves 3 - 4

Try other vegetables and herbs to add a little creativity to your dish. Scrambled tofu goes well on a whole wheat pita with sprouts and tomatoes or with oven fried new potatoes. Served cold it can be a dairy-free egg salad. For a Tex-Mex version garnish the scrambled tofu with Mexican salsa and guacamole or rice sour cream and roll into a whole wheat or corn tortilla.

"Eggless" Tofu Benedict

*This egg and butter-free dish is a healthy and
delicious breakfast or brunch entree.*

Marinated Tofu

1 lb.	Extra Firm Tofu, drained and pressed dry for 1 hour
1/4 cup	Fresh Lemon Juice
1/4 cup	Cold Pressed Olive Oil
1 tb.	Bragg Liquid Amino Acids

Directions

1. Place the tofu on a cutting surface and slice into 4 steaks.
2. Place remaining ingredients in a blender and puree. Pour marinade over the tofu steaks.
3. Preheat oven to the broil setting and 500 degrees. Allow tofu to marinate while heating.
4. Remove tofu from the marinade, place on a sheet pan and broil on the top rack.
5. When the tofu has become somewhat golden in color it is ready to be served.

Assembly Instructions

4 each	Toasted Whole Wheat English Muffins or Whole Wheat Bread Slices
2 each	Vine Ripe Tomatoes, sliced into 1/4 inch slices
4 each	Grilled Tofu Steaks
1 1/2 cups	Mock Bearnaise Sauce, located in sauce chapter

1. Place English muffins or 1 piece of whole wheat bread that is cut in half on a plate.
2. Reheat the tofu steaks if necessary and place one piece over the toasted bread.
3. Place two tomato slices over the tofu steak.
4. Ladle about two ounces of warm Bearnaise sauce over the tomatoes and serve.

Serves 4

Tofu Meatballs

Even those guests who did not like tofu previously have found these tofu meatballs delicious.

2 lb.	Extra firm Tofu, drained and pressed for 1 hour
2 ts.	Olive Oil (or 1/4 cup Vegetable Broth to reduce the fat calories)
1 each	Medium Yellow onion, diced 1/2"
1 each	Medium Red Pepper, Diced 1/2"
1 tb.	Minced Garlic
1 tb.	Oregano, fresh chopped
2 ts.	Thyme leaves
dash	Cayenne Pepper
2 tb.	Low Sodium Tamari or Lite Soy Sauce

Directions

1. While tofu is draining, begin chopping the vegetables.
2. In a saute pan heat oil or broth and saute the vegetables until golden brown.
3. In a mixing bowl, mash or crumble the tofu into small pieces.
4. Add the vegetables and remaining ingredients and mix thoroughly.
5. Preheat oven to 425 degrees.
6. With an ice cream scoop #20 size, pack tofu mixture tightly and place onto a sheet pan that has been lightly oiled with canola oil. Hand-pack the tofu into balls if scoop is unavailable.
7. Bake tofu balls 45 minutes or until well browned and serve with your favorite pasta and sauce or garlic mashed potatoes and gravy.

Serves 4 - 6

Grilled Tofu Steaks

The Bar-B-Que Grill is an important companion in our cuisine.

1 lb. pkg.	Extra Firm Tofu
1/2 cup	Spicy Marinade - Jamaican Jerk (by Troy), Cajun Spice, Oriental Vinaigrette recipe on page 69, or Bar-B-Que Sauce, to name a few

Directions

1. Remove tofu from the container and place in a colander with paper towels. Place towels under and around the tofu and place a melon or other heavy object on top of the tofu and press dry for 1 hour. This will remove most of the liquid from the center of the tofu.
2. Remove tofu and cut horizontally into four slices.
3. Line a casserole with the marinade, place the tofu in and pour more marinade over.
4. Allow tofu to marinate for one hour at room temperature.
5. Heat your grill at its hottest setting for about 5 minutes.
6. Rub the grill irons with a little canola oil and cook tofu on both sides until grill marks appear.
7. Serve with a little of the remaining marinade over the tofu.

Serves 4

Stir-Fried Tofu and Vegetables

1 lb.	Extra Firm Tofu, drain, press and cut into 1 inch cubes *(Try replacing the Tofu with thinly sliced Seitan)*
1/3 cup	Alcohol-free White Wine or Sake
1/3 cup	Low-Sodium Tamari or Soy Sauce
1 ts.	Fresh minced Garlic
1 ts.	Fresh minced Ginger
1/4 cup	Distilled or Pure Water
2-3 tb.	Arrowroot, mix with the water until creamy
1 head	Broccoli, cut into florettes
1 each	Carrot, peeled if not organic, and bias sliced 1/4 inch thick
2 stalks	Bok Choy or Celery, trim outer leaves, bias sliced 1/2 inch
1 each	Red, Orange or Yellow Pepper, cut into 1 inch cubes
1 cup	Snow Peas
1/4 cup	Unsalted Cashews (Optional)
1 cup	Bean Sprouts
3 each	Scallions, slice into 1/2 inch pieces
2 ts.	Toasted Sesame Oil

Directions

1. While tofu is pressing, cut and lightly steam the vegetables. Snow peas cook quickly, so be sure to add them last.
2. In a wok or large pot bring the soy sauce, garlic, wine and ginger to boil.
3. Thicken the sauce with arrowroot mixture. For a sweeter sauce, add some apple juice!
4. Add the tofu, bean sprouts, vegetables and sesame oil, cover and steam until the vegetables are hot but not over cooked.

Serve over brown rice, soba noodles, or rice noodles.

Serves 4 - 6

You can also prepare this recipe the traditional way by heating the sesame oil in a wok. Add the vegetables and stir fry, then add the sauce and tofu. However, we avoid exposing the sesame oil to excessive heat to avoid the hydrogenating of the oil. We add the sesame oil at the end of the cooking process. This ensures that the dish retains its best flavor as well.

Thanksgiving
Turkey Style Tofu Loaf

The freezing of the tofu gives this dish its amazing meatlike texture. The nutritional yeast breading is rich in protein and all of the essential amino acids.

1 Lb.	Extra Firm Tofu
2 qts.	Boiling Water
2/3 cup	Low Sodium Tamari or Low Sodium Soy Sauce
1/2 cup	Nutritional Yeast
1 tb.	Garlic Powder

Directions

1. Drain and press dry the tofu, cover with plastic wrap and freeze.
2. Preheat oven to 375 degrees .
3. Remove Tofu from the freezer and place in boiling water for 5 minutes.
4. Place Tofu in a strainer and press to remove the liquid.
5. Dip the tofu in tamari quickly, rotating from side to side to coat evenly. (The longer you marinate the tofu the saltier it becomes.)
6. Combine the nutritional yeast and garlic powder, add the tofu and coat evenly.
7. Lightly oil a sheet pan with canola oil and bake tofu for 45 minutes or until brown.
8. Remove from oven, slice and serve hot or cold.

Serves 3 - 4

Red Beans and Tofu Enchiladas

If you are trying to get a "reluctant someone" to enjoy tofu for the first time, this could be the perfect dish.

Red Bean Preparation

1 1/2 qts.	Distilled Water
1 cup	Organic Red Beans, soaked in scalding water for 1-2 hours

(If time is a factor you may substitute canned beans. For variety try black beans as well.)

2 each	Bay Leaves
1 tb.	Minced Garlic
2 tb.	Ground Cumin
1/8 ts.	Cayenne Pepper
1 ts.	Sea Salt, Optional

Directions

1. In a large pot bring the distilled water to a boil , strain the beans and add to the pot.
2. Add the bay leaves and boil gently for 1 hour.
3. Add all the remaining ingredients and cook for 1 hour or until beans are tender.
4. Adjust seasonings to your personal taste, strain and set aside beans until cool.

Tofu Preparation
(You will need a 1 lb. package of extra firm tofu)

1. While beans are cooking remove the tofu from its package and drain.
2. In a strainer place the tofu and press down with a heavy object to drain.
3. Allow tofu to drain for about 1 hour. Then cut into 1/2 inch cubes and set aside.

Enchilada Assembly

You will need:

3 oz.   Fat Free Soy Cheddar Cheese, shredded
3 oz.   Fat Free Soy Monterey Jack Cheese with Jalapenos, shredded
1 pkg. Whole Wheat Flour Tortillas, 8 inch size
1 qt.   Enchilada Sauce, recipe on page 190

Directions

1.   Preheat oven to 400 degrees.
2.   In a bowl combine the beans, tofu, two cups of enchilada sauce and half of the cheeses.
3.   Place a tortilla flat on a table and add about one cup of the bean and tofu mix and roll.
4.   In a casserole dish ladle enough of the enchilada sauce in the bottom to coat.
5.   Place the rolled tortillas over the sauce, and cover with the remaining sauce.
6.   Sprinkle the remaining cheese over and bake uncovered for about 20-25 minutes.
7.   Remove from oven and serve hot with Mexican Salsa and Guacamole .

Garnish with black olives and soy sour cream.

Serves 4 - 6

Eggplant Parmesan

This is a much lower-fat, cholesterol-free version.
It is also easier to prepare when you "oven fry" the eggplant.

1 qt.	Whole-Wheat Bread Crumbs
2 tb.	Oregano Flakes
2 cups	Whole-Wheat Flour, or other whole-grain flour
1 1/2 cups	Water
1/2 cup	Egg Replacer
3 each	Eggplant, peel and slice lengthwise 1/2 inch thick
1/3 cup	Canola Oil
2 qts.	Marinara Sauce, recipe on page 194 or your favorite Marinara Sauce recipe
12 oz.	Soy Mozzarella Cheese Fat Free, shredded
1/2 cup	Grated Soy Parmesan Cheese Lite

Tofu Filling

1 1/2 lb.	Firm Tofu drained, pressed dry then mashed
2 tb.	Roasted Sesame Tahini
2 tb.	Yellow Miso
2 tb.	Fresh Basil or Parsley, chopped

Combine ingredients and set aside for future assembly.

Eggplant Parmesan *(continued)*

Directions

1. Preheat oven to 400 degrees.
2. To bread the eggplant: place in a bowl the whole-wheat flour. In a second bowl the Egg Replacer and water mixed together. In the third bowl the whole-wheat bread crumbs and oregano. Now dust the eggplant in the flour, then dip in the wet mixture. Lastly, coat the eggplant with the bread crumbs mix and place on a sheet pan side by side.
3. In a large saute pan lightly coat with canola oil and heat to saute.
4. Pan-fry the eggplant until golden brown and crispy on both sides. *To "oven fry" place on an oiled sheet pan and bake on the bottom rack until bottom is brown, about 20 minutes. Flip over and brown the other side.*
5. In a 8 x 8 casserole spread 1 cup of marinara sauce evenly.
6. Layer over the sauce the eggplant side by side.
7. Place the tofu mixture completely over the eggplant about one half inch thick.
8. Spread 1 cup of marinara sauce over the tofu mix and spread evenly.
9. Cover the tofu with more eggplant, cutting in pieces if necessary to cover completely.
10. Spread two cups marinara sauce over the eggplant.
11. Sprinkle with the soy mozzarella cheese, then the parmesan and bake uncovered for 35-40 minutes or until slightly browned.
12. Remove from oven and cool for 10 minutes before slicing and serve with remaining Marinara Sauce.

Serves 4 - 6

Rice-History and Cooking Techniques

We recommend using brown rice in the recipes in this book, because of its nutritional values. Brown rice results from the first milling of rice when the inedible husk is removed. At this point the brown rice has retained the nutrients, fiber-dense bran and germ. Brown Rice is available in long, medium and short grain. The short grain cooks somewhat stickier and moist. It is more compatible in puddings and casseroles. The longer grains are predominantly used in entrees and side dishes.We do recommend using brown rice within one month of purchase if stored at room temperature. Otherwise, it is best to refrigerate the rice, because the germ is prone to rancidity.

Further milling of rice leads to white rice or polished rice. The polishing removes the bran, germ, fiber, B vitamins, thiamine, and niacine! Enriched white rice, like enriched bread, has had some of the nutrients added back, but not the fiber or trace elements.

Converted rice goes back to World War II when husked rice was parboiled, and dried before milling. In the process, vitamins and minerals in the bran layer are forced into the rice kernel, creating a more nutritious product but one that is not appropriate for most recipes.

Long grain rice - rice that is 4 times longer than it is wide - includes Basmati from India, Jasmine from Thailand, Texmati - a basmati grown in Texas and popcorn and pecan rice from Louisiana, known for its nutty fragrance. Other long grain varieties include red rice, Thai black rice, Lundbergs Wehani - a basmati and red bran rice and Black Japonica - a short grain mahogany and black rice.

The art of cooking rice varies among countries and cuisines. A simple rule of thumb is to always rinse the rice in a strainer first. If the rice is for plain cooked rice, 2 cups of boiling water to 1 cup of dry rice is a good ratio. If you saute onions, garlic or other vegetables before adding the rice and water, a little less than 2 cups of water is necessary. When the water comes to the second boil after the rice has been added, cover and simmer for about 20 minutes. Lower heat to warm, cover rice and allow another 15 minutes for the remaining liquid to evaporate. Some of us like our rice a little firmer than others, so if the rice has come to the tenderness you prefer and the liquid is still present, you may strain the rice quickly and return it to the pot and cover and let rest for about 10 minutes.

I hope this information will give you the confidence to make the correct choices when purchasing and cooking rice.

Rice Entrees

Vegetable Sushi Rolls are healthy, delicious and easy to make; with a little practice.

Florentine Rice

This entree is also delicious served chilled for a cold lunch or buffet salad.

1 ts.	Organic Cold Pressed Olive Oil
1 each	Vidalia Onion, diced 1/2 inch
1 ts.	Minced Garlic
8 oz.	Mushrooms, cut in half
1 each	Red, Yellow or Orange Pepper, diced 1/2 inch (if time allows, roast and peel first before dicing)
1/3 cup	Roasted Pine Nuts, roast at 400 degrees 12-15 minutes on a sheet pan
1/2 cup	Sundried Tomatoes, julienne slices
3 1/2 cups	Distilled or Pure Water, scalding
2 cups	Brown Basmati, Jasmine or other Brown Rice
1 each	Bay Leaf
1 ts.	Sea Salt (Optional)
dash	Cayenne Pepper
4 oz.	Fresh Spinach, cleaned, destemmed and cut leaves in half

Directions

1. In a large pot heat the oil to saute, add onions and garlic until lightly browned. Add mushrooms and simmer.
2. Add remaining ingredients, except the spinach, cover and simmer for 20 minutes.
3. When about 3/4 of the liquid is gone, fold in spinach, lower heat to warm and cover.
3. Serve when rice is tender or water is evaporated. If the rice is tender to your liking before the water is completely gone, place the rice in a strainer to remove the excess water, then return to the pot, cover and hold for service.

Serves 4 - 6

Jambalaya Rice

In this tribute to New Orleans, the seitan and tofu hot dogs replace the ham and sausage!

2 1/2 cups	Brown Basmati Rice or other brown rice
1 qt.	Distilled Water
2 each	Large Vine Ripe tomatoes, cored and diced 1/2 inch or 16 oz. can Muir Glen organic diced tomatoes
2 tb.	Minced Garlic
2 tb.	Cajun Spice
2 each	Bay Leaves
1 each	Vidalia or Yellow Onion, peeled and 1/2 inch dice
1 each	Medium Red Pepper, seeded and 1/2 inch dice
1 each	Medium Yellow or Orange Pepper, 1/2 inch dice
3 each	Tofu Hot Dogs, sliced 1/2 inch
3 oz.pkg.	Bar-B-Que Seitan, cut into 1/2 inch cubes

Directions

1. Bring water to a boil, while waiting, rinse the rice through a strainer for a fluffier rice.
2. When water comes to a boil, add the tomatoes, bay leaf, garlic and Cajun spice.
3. Bring to boil again and add the rice, cover and simmer for 10 minutes.
4. Add the vegetables and continue to simmer covered, while stirring occasionally.
5. After another 10 minutes fold in the Seitan and Tofu Hot Dogs. Cover and cook until the liquid has evaporated.

Serves 4 - 6

Brown Rice and Lentil Stew

This dish serves as a complete protein and is a nice complement to a grilled vegetable platter.

3 qts.	Distilled or Pure Water
1 lb.	Organic Green or Pink Lentils
1 each	Large Vidalia or Yellow Onion, diced 1/2 inch
2 each	Carrots, diced 1/2 inch
3 each	Celery, diced 1/2 inch
1 each	Red Pepper, diced 1/2"
2 each	Bay Leaves
2 tb.	Minced Garlic
1/4 cup	Bragg Liquid Aminos
1 1/2 tb.	Curry Powder
dash	Cayenne Pepper
1 qt.	Cooked Brown Rice
1 cup	Fresh Kale, cut in large pieces

Directions

1. In a large pot, bring the water to a boil. In a bowl, rinse lentils, and strain.
2. Add lentils, cover and simmer for about 30 minutes while stirring occasionally.
3. Skim the foam off of the stock and add the vegetables and spices.
4. Continue to cook, skimming the foam as needed, and stirring often to avoid scorching.
5. When the lentils are tender, add the kale and fold into the cooked brown rice along with some of the lentil stock and serve.

Serves 4 - 6

Red Beans and Rice

When rice and legumes are combined they become a complete protein with all of the essential amino acids.

2 1/2 qts.	Distilled Water
1lb.	Organic Red Beans, soaked in cold water for 1-2 hours

You may substitute any of your favorite beans or lentils for the red beans.
(If time is a factor you may substitute canned beans. Be sure to check sodium content before purchasing canned products.)

2 each	Bay Leaves
2 tb.	Minced Garlic
1 each	Vidalia or Yellow Onion, diced 1/2 inch
1 each	Red Pepper, diced 1/2 inch
1 each	Yellow or Orange pepper, diced 1/2 inch
1 1/2 tb.	Ground Cumin
dash	Cayenne Pepper
2 ts.	Sea Salt, Optional

Directions

1. In a large pot bring the distilled water to a boil , strain the beans and add to the pot.
2. Add the bay leaves and garlic and boil gently for 1 hour.
3. Add all the remaining ingredients and cook for 1 hour or until beans are tender.
4. Adjust seasonings to your personal taste and set aside.

Brown Rice Preparation

3 1/2 cups	Distilled or Pure Water
2 cups	Brown Basmati, Jasmine or other Brown Rice, place in a strainer and rinse with cool water
1 each	Bay Leaf

Directions

1. In a large pot bring the water to a boil and add the rice and the bay leaf.
2. Cover and cook for about 25 minutes or until most of the liquid is gone.
3. Lower heat to simmer and cover until rice is tender or water is evaporated.
4. When the beans are tender fold into the rice adding a little of the bean broth until the proper consistency of rice to beans is attained.

Serves 6 - 8

Southwestern Rice

This dish is great as a hot entree or as a chilled salad!

2 cups	Brown Basmati Rice
3 1/2 cups	Distilled Water
1 ts.	Saffron threads or Tumeric
1 each	Bay Leaf
1/2 ts.	Sea Salt, Optional
1 1/2 tb.	Chili Powder
1 cup	Cooked Black Beans, drained in a strainer
1 cup	Yellow Corn, cut from cob or frozen and steamed
1/2 bunch	Cilantro, chopped finely
1 1/2 cups	Mexican Salsa, recipe on page 195

Directions

1. Bring water to a boil, add bay leaf, saffron, chili powder and rice.
2. Cover and cook 30 - 40 minutes or until most all the liquid is gone.
3. Turn off heat, cover and hold until all liquid evaporates.
4. Heat the black beans, corn, cilantro and salsa fold into the rice, adjust seasoning as desired and serve hot.

Serves 6 - 8

Vegetable Sushi Rolls

This versatile dish can be served as an entree, appetizer, hors d'euvre or snack.

3 3/4 cups	Pure or Distilled water
2 cups	Medium Brown Rice, Basmati Rice is the superior rice, if available
1 ts.	Sea Salt, optional
1 bunch	Scallions, cut in 1/4 inch slices
2 tb.	Ume Plum Paste (optional ingredient), be aware of the high sodium content
2 each	Carrots, peeled if not organic and hand-grated or shredded in a food processor
1 each	Cucumber, peeled, cut in half lengthwise, and remove seeds with a spoon or Parisienne scoop. Now cut into long julienne strips lengthwise, 1/2 inch thick 1 each Red Pepper, cut in half, seeded and sliced into julienne strips
1 each	Ripe Avocado, cut in half, remove seed and peel, then julienne in 1/2 inch slices
1 pint	Alfalfa Sprouts
1 pkg.	Sushi Nori Sheets
1 each	Bamboo Sushi Rolling Mat

Sushi assembly instructions are on the next two pages.

Vegetable Sushi
Directions

1. Bring water and salt to a boil, meanwhile place rice in a strainer and rinse with cool water. Add rice to the pot and cover. Boil gently for 20-25 minutes, when most of the water is evaporated, lower heat to low, cover until water is absorbed.
2. Remove the rice from the pot, place into a large bowl and fold in the plum paste and scallions.
3. Allow rice to cool at room temperature. While the rice is cooling prepare the vegetables.
4. To assemble, on a clean counter top place all the cut vegetables and rice at the top of the table. Place a bowl of cool water to the side for dipping your fingers when they get starchy and to seal the ends of the nori rolls later in the process.
5. Place the sushi mat in front of you horizontally, then place 1 sushi nori sheet, shiny side down, on the mat. Be sure the horizontal lines in the nori sheets are placed horizontally the same as the bamboo mat.
6. Spoon the rice mixture about 1/2 inch thick evenly over the nori sheet. Omit about 1 inch on the nori sheet closest to you and 2 inches farthest from you without rice. Refer to the sushi rolling diagram.
7. Along the center of the rice spread evenly 1/4 of the carrots and vegetables, allowing the vegetables to extend slightly past the end of the nori sheets.
8. To roll: begin rolling the part of the mat closest to you with both hands one quarter of a turn to cover the vegetables in the center. Grasp the mat firmly with both hands to secure the roll. With your left hand hold the part of the mat farthest from you. With the right hand holding the vegetable roll part tug slightly to tighten the roll. Complete the rolling slowly with both hands, tugging from time to time as previously to further tighten the roll.
9 . Dip your fingers in the water and seal horizontally along the end of the roll. Allow to dry. (**Repeat steps 4-8 with the remaining products.)**
10. To Slice: Use a long sharp slicing knife. Trim the ends of the roll then cut into your favorite shapes, whether it be 1 inch slices or vary with a diagonal cut on one side and a straight cut on the other side to give the rolls different heights and angles.

Serve with carrot ginger sauce, wasabi, pickled ginger and or low-sodium soy sauce or tamari.

Makes 3 - 4 rolls, with 5 - 6 cuts per roll

Step-by-Step: Rolling Sushi

 1. Wet your fingers with cold water and press the rice onto the nori, making a 1/2 inch-thick layer that covers the sheet from side to side. Across the top, leave a 1/2-inch strip of nori exposed.

 2. If using wasabi dab a little of the paste along the length of the rice, about 1/2 inch above the bottom edge of the nori. Place the filling on the rice. Lift up the bottom of the mat, rolling the rice over the filling. Use your fingers to keep the filling in place.

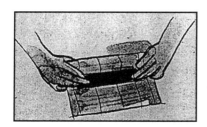

3. Keep rolling away from you until the bottom edge of the nori meets the top side of the nori just where the rice ends.

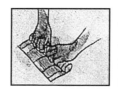 4. Unroll the mat and push the roll forward slightly so that the seam faces the mat. Lift the mat over the roll and move your hands along the length of the mat, pressing the roll and compacting it as evenly as possible.

5. Just before serving, dip a sharp knife in cold water and cut each roll into 1-inch lengths.

Brown Rice Pilaf

This recipe can be made even easier by placing all ingredients in a covered casserole and baking at 400 degrees for one hour or until liquid is evaporated.

1 1/2 cups	Brown Basmati Rice or other brown rice
2 3/4 cups	Distilled or Pure Water
3 each	Scallions, sliced 1/4 " thick
1 each	Red or Yellow Pepper, diced 1/2"
2 each	Celery Stalk, julenne and dice 1/2 inch
1 each	Bay Leaf
1/2 cup	Roasted Almonds or unsalted Cashew nuts
1/2 cup	Raisins
dash	Cayenne Pepper

Directions

1. Rinse the rice in a strainer and remove the dark kernels.
2. Bring water to a boil, add rice and bay leaf, stir, cover and lower heat to a simmer.
3. While rice is cooking cut the vegetables. After 15-20 minutes add the vegetables.
4. Simmer the vegetables 5 minutes, add the cayenne, almonds and raisins.
5. When most of the liquid is gone and rice is tender, turn off the heat, cover and allow to rest 10-15 minutes until moisture has evaporated before serving.

Serves 6 - 8

Potato Entrees

Shepherd's Pie

We have revived an old favorite by using textured vegetable protein products or crumbled Boca Burgers in place of meat products.

Garlic Mashed New Potatoes

Having always been a mashed potato lover, this is one of my favorite recipes.

8 each	Medium Red Potatoes, scrubbed and quartered with the skin on
1 1/2 cups	Rice Milk, scalded
1 1/2 tb.	Minced Garlic
1 ts.	Sea Salt, optional
dash	Cayenne Pepper
1 tb.	Chopped Parsley, optional
2/3 cup	Soy Parmesan Cheese (Optional)

Directions

1. Bring a pot of water to a boil, add the potatoes and cook until tender.
2. Strain the potatoes, transfer to a sturdy bowl and mash with the rice milk.
3. Add the next 4 ingredients to the potatoes while mashing.
4. Preheat the oven to the broil setting at 500 degrees.
5. With a paper towel and canola oil, lightly oil the bottom of a casserole or sheet pan.
6. Spread the mashed potatoes evenly throughout the casserole and smooth out the top with a spatula.
7. Sprinkle the soy parmesan cheese over the potatoes, place on top oven rack and gratinee about 1 minute until brown.
8. Cut the potatoes with a knife and remove from the pan with a spatula.

Serves 4 - 6

Sweet Potato Souffle

*This egg-free souffle can be enjoyed year round. You may not be able to wait
for a holiday to come once you have tried this recipe.*

4 each	Large Sweet Potatoes, peeled and cut into quarters
2/3 cup	Rice Dream or Almond Milk, Scalded
2 tb.	Fruit Source Sweetener, available in natural food stores
1/2 cup	Brown Rice Syrup, warm
2 ts.	Ground Cinnamon
1 ts.	Ground Nutmeg
1 cup	Organic Oatmeal Flakes
2/3 cup	Chopped Pecans

Directions

1. Bring a pot of water to a boil and cook the potatoes until they are very tender.
2. Preheat oven to 400 degrees.
3. Drain the potatoes and transfer to a large mixing bowl.
4. Mash the potatoes with the Rice Dream, Fruit Source and half of the cinnamon and nutmeg.
5. Place potato mixture in a casserole dish and smooth over with a spatula.
6. In a bowl toss the remaining cinnamon and nutmeg with the pecans and oatmeal.
7. Add about 1/2 cup of Brown Rice Syrup to the nut mix and spread evenly over the potatoes. If you desire a sweeter topping, add more syrup.
8. Bake for about 35 - 40 minutes on the top rack or until the topping is a little brown and crispy.

Serves 4 - 6

Potato Latkes *(Pancakes)*

Traditionally served for Hanukkah, but in our home we had them on many Friday nights.

3 each	Idaho Potatoes, peeled and grated on the larger grate size

Place the shredded potatoes in cool water to prevent discoloration, before proceeding.

1 each	Small Yellow Onion, grated on the fine grate size (Optional)
3 each	Scallions, sliced 1/4 inch
3 tb.	Whole-Wheat Flour
1 ts.	Fresh Minced Garlic
1/2 ts.	Sea Salt, optional
dash	Cayenne Pepper
1/4 cup	Canola Oil

Directions

1. Drain and press the potatoes until very dry.
2. In a large bowl, toss the potatoes and all the ingredients except the canola oil.
3. In a large saute pan, heat the oil to medium high.
4. Form the potatoes into patties and fry until crispy on both sides.
5. Place the potatoes on a paper towel and blot off the excess oil on both sides.
6. Serve hot or reheat later in a 400 degree oven.

Yield is about 8 pancakes, depending on the size
Serve with organic apple sauce and soy sour cream.

You may question, *"Is this a low fat recipe"*?
There are occasions in life where we need to celebrate. I think moderation is the key to happiness and a healthy mind and body! For a lower fat alternative, try brushing a pan with canola oil, place the pancakes on the pan, and bake at 425 degrees until brown on the bottom. Flip the pancakes over and bake another 10-15 minutes until crispy on both sides.

Curried New Potatoes and Garbanzo Beans

This legume and vegetable stew is high in protein
and has a variety of different flavor sensations.

1 tb.	Canola or Peanut Oil
1 each	Vidalia Onion, diced 1/2 inch
1 each	Red Pepper, diced 1/2 inch
1 tb.	Minced Garlic
2 tb.	Curry Powder
2 tb.	Whole Wheat Flour
1 ts.	Ground Cumin
1/2 ts.	Sea Salt
dash	Cayenne Pepper
2 1/2 cups	Pure or Distilled Water
2 cups	Red Potatoes, quartered with the skin on
2 cups	Cooked Garbanzo Beans
1 each	Red Delicious or Golden Apple, diced 1/2 inch
1 tb.	Lemon Juice, toss with the cut apples to avoid discoloring
1 cup	Frozen Baby Peas
4 cups	Cooked Brown Rice (Optional)

Directions

1. Heat oil in a large pan to saute. Add onions, peppers and garlic and brown lightly.
2. Fold in the flour and spices thoroughly with the heat on low.
3. Add the water to the vegetables, raise heat and stir until thickened.
4. Add potatoes, beans and apples and cook covered until the potatoes are tender.
5. Fold in the frozen peas, adjust spices as needed and serve as is or over brown rice.

Serves 3 - 4

Twice Stuffed Baked Potato

A Tempeh product "Fakin Bacon" and Soy or Rice Sour Cream,
makes this as tasty, yet healthier than the original version.

3 each	Large Idaho Baking Potatoes, rinsed and scrubbed
6 each	Red Bliss Potatoes, scrubbed and quartered
2 quarts	Pure or Distilled Water
1 cup	Rice Dream or Soy Milk, Scalded
4 each	Scallions, sliced 1/4 inch
1 tb.	Minced Garlic
1/2 ts.	Sea Salt
dash	Cayenne Pepper
3 tb.	Soy Sour Cream, optional
4 pieces	"Fakin Bacon", bake until crispy and chopped
1 cup	Fat Free Soy Cheddar Cheese, shredded
2 tb.	Grated Soy Parmesan Cheese, optional

Directions

1. Preheat oven to 400 degrees. Place Idaho potatoes in oven and bake for 1 hour.
2. Set baked potatoes aside to cool, meanwhile bringing water to a boil.
3. Boil the red bliss potatoes until very tender, strain water and return potatoes to the pot or mixing bowl.
4. Cut the baked potatoes lengthwise and scoop out the pulp.
5. Add the potato pulp, rice dream, Fakin Bacon, soy sour cream and spices to the red potato mix and mash with a potato masher.
6. Fill the baked potato shells with the potato mix and top with the cheeses.
7. Bake 18-20 minutes or until cheese is melted and serve hot.

Serves 6

Oven Browned
Herbed New Potatoes

These potatoes are great for breakfast, lunch or dinner.

8 each	Medium Red Bliss a.k.a. New Potatoes
1/4 cup	Organic Cold Pressed Olive Oil
2 ts.	Minced Garlic
2 tb.	Chopped Parsley
1 tb.	Fresh chopped Thyme or Rosemary
1/2 ts.	Sea Salt, optional
2/3 cup	Grated Soy Parmesan Cheese

Directions

1. Preheat oven to 425 degrees.
2. Scrub potatoes under cold running water. Cut in quarters and hold in cool water.
3. In a blender, whip together olive oil and spices. Drain potatoes thoroughly in a colander.
4. Toss oil mixture with potatoes and lay potatoes on a sheet pan.
5. Bake for about 45 minutes to an hour, remove from oven and sprinkle with cheese. Return to the top rack of the oven for about 10 minutes or until the cheese is lightly browned and crispy.

Serves 3 - 4

Oven Fried Sweet Potato Spears

Caution: *It is a good idea to prepare extra or you may run out quickly!*

4 each	Medium Sweet Potatoes, do not peel
1/4 cup	Organic Cold Pressed Olive Oil
1 ts.	Minced Garlic
2 ts.	Fresh chopped Thyme or Rosemary
2 ts.	Fresh chopped Basil or Oregano

Directions

1. Preheat oven to 425 degrees.
2. Scrub sweet potatoes under cold running water. Cut in half lengthwise, then cut in wedges 3/4 inch thick.
3. Whip together olive oil and herb mixture in a blender or in a bowl.
4. Toss oil mixture with sweet potatoes, reserve remaining oil for later use and place potatoes on a sheet pan.
5. Bake for 45 minutes to an hour on the top rack or until tender and a little charred.

For a more caramelized flavor bake longer, being careful not to burn.

Serves 4

• •

Baked Home Fried Potatoes

This recipe is much lower in fat than traditional "home fries". It goes well with scrambled tofu or any steamed or grilled vegetables.

1 1/2 lbs.	New Potatoes, a.k.a. Red Bliss Potatoes, scrub and quarter
2 each	Medium Yellow Onions, cut in half and sliced into 1/4 inch slices
1 tb.	Minced Garlic
1/4 cup	Low-Sodium Tamari or Low-Sodium Soy Sauce
dash	Cayenne Pepper

Directions

1. Preheat oven to 425 degrees and bring a pot of water to a boil.
2. Parcook the potatoes in water about 10 minutes, then place in strainer to drain thoroughly.
3. In a bowl blend the tamari, pepper and garlic.
4. In a large bowl toss the potatoes, onions and tamari mix.
5. Brush a sheet pan with canola oil and layer with the potatoes.
6. Bake for 35 - 40 minutes on the top rack or until slightly crispy.

Serves 4 - 6

Potatoes Oreganato

This easy-to-prepare recipe can be ready in less than 45 minutes.

3 each	Idaho Potatoes, scrubbed and sliced lenghthwise into 1/2 inch slices
1 1/2 cups	Whole-Wheat Bread Crumbs
2 tb.	Organic Virgin Olive Oil
2 ts.	Minced Garlic
1 tb.	Oregano Leaves
2 ts.	Ground Oregano
1/2 ts.	Sea Salt, optional
dash	Cayenne Pepper

Directions

1. Preheat oven to 400 degrees.
2. Slice potatoes and hold in cold water until needed. Drain in a strainer before using.
3. Combine bread crumbs and remaining ingredients in a mixing bowl.
4. Place a sliced potato in your hand and sprinkle generously with the bread crumb topping.
5. Place the potato on an oiled sheet pan. Repeat with the remaining potatoes, placing them side by side on the pan.
6. Bake on the top rack of the oven about 25 minutes until the crumbs are browned and the potatoes are tender.
7. Remove potatoes from the oven and lift from the pan with a metal spatula to serve.

Serves 3 - 4

Shepherd's Pie

You will love this Vegan twist to an old favorite;
cholesterol-free and much lower in fat calories.

1 1/2 lb.	Boca Burgers, Gimme Lean or Morningstar Meat-Style products, crumble before coking
1 ts.	Canola Oil or 1/4 cup Vegetable Broth
1 each	Large Yellow Onion, diced 1/2 inch
1 each	Red Pepper, diced 1/2 inch
2 ts.	Minced Garlic
dash	Cayenne Pepper
2 tb.	Vegetable Broth, Jensen's or Dr. Bonners Brand mix with 1/2 cup water
2 cups	Cooked Corn Kernels

Mashed Potato Topping

6 each	Large Red Potatoes, quartered with the skin on
1 cup	Rice Dream or Soy Milk, scalded
1 ts.	Sea Salt, optional
1 tb.	Minced Garlic
dash	Cayenne Pepper
	Paprika

Shepherd's Pie *(continued)*

Directions

1. Heat oil in a large saute pan add the onions and garlic and brown slightly.
2. Add the Boca Burger, red peppers and vegetable broth, simmer 10 minutes, then add the corn and cover and hold on warm setting.
3. While the Boca Burger is cooking, bring a pot of water to a boil and cook the potatoes until tender.
4. Drain the potatoes and add the Rice Dream and seasonings and mash thoroughly.
5. Preheat oven to 400 degrees.
6. Spread the Boca Burger mix evenly in a casserole and cover with the mashed potatoes.

   If you have a pastry bag and a large rosette tip you can also garnish the potatoes around the perimeter of the pan.
7. Dust the top with paprika and bake on the top rack about 35 - 40 minutes or until slightly browned.
8. Remove from the oven and serve hot, cutting with a metal spatula for uniformity.

Serves 4 - 6

If this recipe is too hearty, try parcooked broccoli and carrot pieces instead of the Boca Burger.

Low Fat Baked Potato Skins

This is a much healthier, lower fat version of the popular fried potato skins.

4 each	Idaho Baking Potatoes
4 oz.	Fat Free Soy Cheddar or Mozzarella Cheese, shredded
3/4 cup	Crispy Tempeh or Fakin' Bacon Pieces, Optional
1/2 cup	Soy Sour Cream or Rice Sour Cream, optional
1/2 bunch	Scallions, cleaned and sliced 1/8 inch

Directions

1. Preheat oven to 400 degrees.
2. Scrub potatoes and place on oven rack directly and bake for 1 hour.
3. Remove potatoes to cool and begin shredding the cheese and slicing scallions. Bake the Fakin' Bacon strips until crispy.
4. Cut the potatoes in half lengthwise to resemble boats and scoop out 2/3 of the pulp.
5. On a sheet pan lay the potato skins side down and sprinkle with the tempeh pieces and cover generously with cheese.
6. Return to oven and bake on top rack 8-10 minutes or until the cheese melts.
7. Garnish with scallions and serve with soy or rice sour cream.

Serves 3 - 4

Ethnic & Miscellaneous Entrees

Vegetable Quesadillas

Made with fat-free soy cheeses and grilled vegetables with roasted peppers. Southwestern Cuisine is alive and well "Vegan Style."

Grilled Vegetable Burritos

One of our most requested entrees. You may want to prepare extras.

1 each	Large Zucchini, sliced 1/2" thick on a bias
1 each	Large Yellow Squash, sliced 1/2" thick on a bias
2 each	Portabella Mushrooms, rinsed and destemmed, with a spoon scrape off the gills on the underside
1 ts.	Minced Garlic
1/3 cup	Organic Cold Pressed Olive Oil
1 ts.	Oregano Leaves
Dash	Cayenne Pepper
1 each	Large Red Pepper, roasted and skinned, cut in 1 inch strips
4 oz.	Fat Free Monterey Jack Soy Cheese, shredded
4 oz.	Fat Free Soy Cheddar Cheese with jalapenos, shredded
6 each	Whole-Wheat Flour Tortillas

Directions

1. Turn on your Bar-B-Que Grill to high heat, preheat the oven to 400 degrees.
2. Blend olive oil, garlic and oregano and brush onto the vegetables.
3. Grill the vegetables on both sides until grill marks occur, and set aside.
4. Roast the pepper, skin side down, on the grill until most of the skin is black. Place peppers in a plastic bag to steam, when cooled, remove and peel away the skin.
5. Slice vegetables in one inch by four inch slices. Begin shredding the cheeses and set aside.

If you prefer to use your oven instead of the grill, turn oven to broil at 500 degrees place the vegetables on a sheet pan and broil on the top rack until lightly browned on one side.

Grilled Vegetable Burritos *(continued)*

Burrito Assembly Instructions

1.   Preheat oven to 400 degrees.
2.   Place the tortilla on a flat surface, sprinkle the cheese evenly over the tortilla.
3.   Place 2 slices of each vegetable along the center of the tortilla from end to end, leave about 1 inch of tortilla empty at the bottom.
4.   Add a slice of the red peppers from end to end over the vegetables.
5.   With the vegetables facing vertically fold the bottom part of the tortilla 1 inch over.
7.   Starting from either side, roll the end of one side of tortilla over the vegetables, continue to roll the tortilla rather tightly until closed.
        Repeat with the remaining tortillas.
8.   Place burritos in a casserole lined with baking paper to prevent sticking. Cover with foil and bake 15 minutes or until the cheese is melted.

Serve with guacamole, Mexican salsa, refried beans or soy sour cream.

1 Burrito per person will serve 6

For a more traditional style burrito, replace the grilled vegetables with meatless chili, recipe on page 140 and/or refried beans.

Stuffed Cabbage Roll (Golomki)

Being Polish and dining on my mother's delicious "Golomki" was a meal I will cherish forever. When my mother asked me if I had a meatless recipe for her classic specialty, I felt it to be an honor to re-create it "Vegan Style".

1 each	Large Green Cabbage, remove core and rinse
1 lb.	Gimme Lean, Morningstar or, if using Vegan Boca Burgers, crumble before using
2 ts.	Cold Pressed Virgin Olive Oil
1 each	Large Vidalia or Yellow Onion
1 each	Red Pepper, diced 1/2 inch
1 tb.	Minced Garlic
12 oz. can	Muir Glen Organic Diced Tomatoes, or fresh diced tomatoes
12 oz. can	Muir Glen Organic Tomato Puree
2 tb.	Fresh Basil Leaves, chopped coarse
2 each	Bay Leaf
1/2 cup	Brown Rice Syrup, optional
dash	Cayenne Pepper
1/2 ts.	Sea Salt, optional
1 cup	Cooked Brown Rice, 1 cup of water to 1/2 cup of rice and cook 30 -35 minutes

Stuffed Cabbage Roll *(con't)*

Directions

1. Place the cabbage and about 1 quart of hot water in a large deep pot. Cover and steam on high heat for about 30 minutes until the cabbage is tender. Place the cabbage carefully in a strainer and allow to cool while preparing the other ingredients.

2. Oil a saute pan and cook the meat substitute until fully cooked, much like ground beef.

3. In a large pot heat the olive oil and lightly brown the onions, garlic and peppers.

4. Add the tomato products and spices and cook 20-30 minutes until flavors have been blended. Adjust seasonings to suit your personal tastes.

5. Transfer the cooked meat product to a large bowl and fold in 1 cup of the tomato sauce and the cooked rice. Allow to cool slightly.

6. Preheat the oven to 400 degrees. Place about 1 1/2 cups of tomato sauce in the bottom of a 9 x 12 inch casserole dish.

7. Gently remove the cabbage leaves one at a time until leaves are too small to use for stuffing. You may julienne the remaining cabbage and add to the side of the casserole.

8. Place one cabbage leaf on the work table and spoon about 1/3 cup of the rice mixture in the center of the leaf. Starting nearest you, begin to roll, while also tucking the outside leaves to close around the filling. When fully rolled place it in the casserole, being sure to keep the loosened part on the bottom of the pan, to ensure they do not open.

9. Complete remaining cabbage rolls, place side by side in the casserole and cover with some of the tomato sauce.

10. Cover the casserole dish with plastic wrap, then with foil and bake 45 minutes until well steamed.

Serves 4 - 6

Serve with remaining sauce. Leftovers may be frozen for a later date and reheated with no loss of quality.

Vegetable Chili

This is one of my favorite chilis to prepare. It tastes even better the next day.

1 tb.	Organic Olive Oil
2 each	Yellow or Vidalia Onions, peeled and cut into 1 inch cubes
2 tb.	Minced Garlic
2 each	Red Peppers, seeded and cut into 1 inch cubes
2 each	Yellow or Orange Peppers, cut into 1 inch cubes
	If time allows, try roasting the peppers first for better flavor
1 each	Small Eggplant, cut into 1 inch cubes, for color and texture, leave the skin on
2 each	Zucchini, cut off ends, split down the middle and cut into 1 inch cubes
2 each	Yellow Squash , cut off ends, split down the middle and cut into 1 inch cubes
3 each	Large Vine Ripe Tomatoes, cored and diced or 1 can Organic Diced Tomatoes (16 oz.)
1 can	Organic Tomato Puree (12 oz.)
3 tb.	Chili Powder
1 tb.	Ground Cumin
1 bunch	Fresh Chopped Cilantro
2 each	Bay Leaves
1 ts.	Sea Salt, optional
1 each	Jalapeno Pepper, remove seeds, chopped very fine
1 can	Kidney or Pinto Beans, strain the liquid and set aside
1 can	Cooked Black Beans, strain the liquid and set aside

Vegetable Chili *(continued)*

Directions

1. Rinse and cut all vegetables and herbs and set aside.
2. In a large pot heat the olive and saute the onions and garlic to a golden brown.
3. Add the peppers, eggplant and squash and continue cooking until slightly tender.
4. Add the tomato products, herbs and spices and continue cooking until well blended.
5. Fold in the beans, cover and simmer for 30-45 minutes.
6. Adjust seasonings as necessary and stir on occasion.

We always use dry organic beans and cook and season our beans. The canned beans will save you a great deal of time and effort. This vegetable stew is wonderful with grilled Corn Bread and Brown Rice Pilaf or try with melted soy cheese. It will hold well 5 -7 days under refrigeration.

Serves 6 - 8

"Meatless" Chili

The day we prepared this chili for the first time, the entire kitchen and our resident taste tester Julio DiIorio looked at each other in amazement; like we had discovered the Vegetarian Holy Grail! Chili was once again back in our lives.

1 tb.	Cold Pressed Virgin Olive Oil or 1/4 cup Water
1 each	Yellow Onion, diced 1/2 inch
1 each	Red Pepper, diced
1 each	Yellow Pepper, diced
1 tb.	Minced Garlic
1 1/2 lb.	Boca Burgers, Gimme Lean or Morningstar Meatstyle products, crumble before cooking
12 oz. can	Muir Glen Organic Diced Tomatoes, or fresh diced tomatoes
1 cup	Muir Glen Organic Tomato Puree
12 oz. can	Cooked Pinto or Kidney Beans, drained
dash	Cayenne Pepper or 1 chopped Jalapeno Pepper
3 tb.	Chili Powder
2 ts.	Ground Cumin
1 ts.	Ground Oregano
1 each	Bay Leaf

Directions

1. Place oil or water in a large saute pan and saute the onions, garlic and pepper. Add the crumbled meat replacement until heated.
2. Add the remaining ingredients, cover and simmer for about 1 hour. Adjust seasoning to suit your personal taste.

Serves 6 - 8

This chili can be served as an entree, as part of a taco salad bar with tortilla chips, as a topping for pizzas, or as a filling for burritos, tacos, enchiladas or wherever your creativity will take you.

Falafel Sandwich

In Israel, falafel is a snack as common as popcorn or ice cream. Falafel is a fried garbanzo bean patty. It has come to mean both the pita sandwich and the patty. We will suggest a low-fat cooking method by oven frying the patties.

2 cups	Cooked Garbanzo Beans, or Chic Peas, if canned use the low sodium brand
1 ts.	Toasted Sesame Oil
1 each	Small Vidalia or Yellow Onion
1 tb.	Minced Garlic
1/3 cup	Soy Yogurt or Soy Sour Cream
2 tb.	Stoneground Mustard
1 1/4 cups	Whole Wheat Bread Crumbs, set aside 1 cup
2 tb.	Fresh Chopped Parsley
1 tb.	Bragg Liquid Aminos
1/2 ts.	Ground Cumin
1/4 ts.	Paprika
Dash	Cayenne Pepper

Directions

1. Drain the beans and reserve the liquid.
2. Heat a saute pan with sesame oil and brown the onions and garlic lightly.
3. Place all ingredients in a food processor or blender and chop coarsely.
   Do not puree the beans totally, allow for that coarser texture.
4. Refrigerate the mix for 20-30 minutes and preheat oven to 425 degrees.
5. When the mix has cooled form into 1/2 inch thick patties. The width of the patty can be 2 inches wide or can be made to fit the size of the pita bread when cut in half. Coat patties with bread crumbs that were set aside.
6. Oil a sheet pan with canola oil, place the patties and bake on the bottom rack about 25 minutes until crispy on the bottom. Remove from oven, flip the patties and bake 15 minutes until crispy on both sides.

Makes 8 - 10 patties

Serve on a whole wheat pita with lettuce, tomato and basil tahini or mustard tahini dressing.

Savory Lentil Loaf

This healthier version of meat loaf is low-fat, high-protein and full of flavor.

2 cups	Pure or Distilled Water
1 cup	Green or Pink Lentils, rinsed
2 tb.	Bragg Liquid Aminos
2 ts.	Ground Cumin
dash	Cayenne Pepper
1 ts.	Canola Oil or 1/4 cup of Water or Broth
1 each	Vidalia or Yellow Onion, diced 1/2 inch
1 each	Red Pepper, diced 1/2 inch
1 tb.	Minced Garlic
3/4 cup	Cooked Brown Rice
3/4 cup	Organic Oatmeal Flakes
2/3 cup	Cooked cut Corn, drained

Directions

1. Place water, lentils and spices in a pot and bring to a medium boil.
2. Cook lentils until tender and the liquid has evaporated. Place the canola oil in a saute pan.
3. Heat the canola and brown the onions. Add the garlic and peppers and cook until tender.
4. Place the lentils, vegetables and remaining ingredients in a large bowl and mix together.
5. Preheat oven to 375 degrees. Oil a loaf pan completely with canola oil.
6. Pack the lentil mixture evenly into the loaf pan and bake for 35-40 minutes.
7. Remove from oven and insert a knife around the edge of the lentil loaf and trim around the pan for easy removal. Invert the pan onto a cutting board, slice into 3/4 inch slices and serve.

Serve with marinara, wild mushroom or roasted red pepper sauce.

Serves 4

Organic Grains and Greens

This protein-packed entree is also extremely low in fat calories.

5 cups	Pure or Distilled Water
1/2 cup	Kamut
1/2 cup	Wheat Berries
1/2 cup	Spelt Berries
1/2 cup	Quinoa
1 tb.	Canola Oil or 1/4 cup of Water or Broth
2 each	Vidalia or Yellow Onions, diced 1/2 inch
2 tb.	Minced Garlic
2 tb.	Curry Powder
1 ts.	Thai Chili Paste
2 tb.	Bragg Liquid Aminos
1/2 ts.	Sea Salt, optional
1 pkg.	Fresh Spinach, remove stems and cut or tear into smaller pieces
1 bx.	Frozen chopped Collard Greens, thaw and press dry in a strainer

Directions

1. Place water in a large pot and bring to a boil.
2. Combine kamut, wheat and spelt berries in a strainer and rinse.
3. Add the 3 grains to the boiling water, cover and cook on medium for 20 minutes.
4. Rinse the quinoa thoroughly in a fine strainer and add to the grains and cook 15 minutes.
5. While the grains are cooking, cut the vegetables.
6. Heat the canola oil in a saute pan and brown the onions, then the garlic.
7. Dissolve the chili paste in the bragg liquid, and add all ingredients to the grains.
8. When the majority of the liquid has evaporated and the berries are tender, lower the heat to warm. Adjust spices as desired, cover and hold hot until served.

Serves 4

Vegetable Pita Pizza

This low-fat recipe will appeal to the kids and the adults as well.
You better be prepared to make more, these pizzas are too good to be low-fat.

1/2 pkg.	Large 8-inch Whole Wheat Pita Bread, if unavailable the smaller size is fine, or use the Focaccia dough recipe on page 210
1/4 cup	Organic Olive Oil
2 ts.	Minced Garlic
2 ts.	Oregano Leaves
4 each	Large Vine Ripe Tomatoes, diced 1/2 inch
Dash	Cayenne Pepper
1 pkg.	Spinach or 1 head Romaine or Escarole Leaves, destemmed, rinsed and drain
8 oz.	Mushrooms, washed and sliced 1/4 inch slices
1 can	Artichoke Hearts, drained and sliced (Optional)
12 oz.	Soy Mozzarella, Fat Free if available, shredded

Directions

1. Preheat oven 400 degrees.
2. Split the Pita in halves with a serrated knife, to resemble a pizza shell.
3. Puree the olive oil and half of the garlic and oregano.
4. With a pastry brush, brush the inside of the pita lightly with the olive oil mix.
5. Bake the pita on a sheet pan for 6 - 8 minutes until golden brown and crispy. Set aside to cool.
6. Combine the tomatoes with the remaining garlic, oregano and cayenne.
7. Lay the pita on a clean table and with the inside half facing upward, cover completely with the spinach leaves. Now add a layer of mushrooms, tomatoes, then artichokes.
8. Cover with soy mozzarella and bake 8-10 minutes on the top oven rack or until cheese is melted completely.

Serves 4 - 6
Other suggestions to create your own personalized gourmet pizza!
Sundried Tomatoes, Imported Sliced Olives, Roasted Red Peppers, Sauteed Onions,
Sauteed Wild Mushrooms, Grilled Eggplant or Meatless Chili

Portabella Mushroom Burger

The Portabella Mushroom is very large and the texture
allows it to make a great sandwich.

1/4 cup	Cold Pressed Extra Virgin Olive Oil
1 each	Small Red or Yellow Pepper
1 ts.	Minced Garlic
1 ts.	Fresh Chopped Thyme or Rosemary Leaves
dash	Cayenne Pepper
4 each	Portabella Mushrooms, destemmed and rinsed well
4 each	Seven-Grain Roll or Focaccia
4 each	Romaine Leaves
4 each	Large Vine Ripe Tomato slices
1 each	Red Onion, sliced thin
1 each	Roasted Yellow or Red Pepper, skinned and quartered

Directions

1. Prepare barbecue on high heat. For added flavor add some soaked mesquite chips.
2. In a blender puree the first five ingredients.
3. With a small spoon, scoop out the gills on the underside of the mushroom cap. Brush both sides of mushrooms with the herb puree.
4. Grill mushrooms until tender, 3-4 minutes on each side.
5. Toast the buns and serve with the mushrooms, vegetables and Basil Mustard Sauce, Salsa Verde, or any of your favorite condiments.

Serves up to 4

Quinoa Pilaf

Quinoa is the oldest grain known to man, dating back to the Aztec Indians. A very rich source of protein, it is prepared just like rice would be but in slightly less time. You can add cooked beans to quinoa the same as you would rice.

1 1/2 cups	Organic Quinoa
2 3/4 cups	Distilled Water
2 each	Scallions, sliced 1/4 " thick
1/2 each	Red Peppers, diced 1/2"
1/2 each	Yellow Peppers, diced 1/2"
1 each	Bay Leaf
1 ts.	Sea Salt (Optional)
dash	Cayenne Pepper or 1 tb. Cajun Spice

Directions

1. Rinse the Quinoa in a strainer to remove the Saponin (soap-like) coating.
2. Bring water to a boil, add Quinoa, salt and bay leaf, stir, cover and simmer 10 minutes.
3. While Quinoa is cooking cut the vegetables, add vegetables and cook 10 minutes.
4. When most of the liquid is gone and Quinoa is tender, turn off the heat, adjust spices, and keep covered until ready to serve.

Serves 4

Mexican Lasagne

You will be amazed at how delicious and simple this Lasagne is to prepare. While very low in fat calories, it also cooks in 1/3 the time of traditional Lasagne.

1 each	8 x 8 inch casserole
3 cups	Refried Beans, recipe on page 150
2 pkgs.	Organic White, Blue or Yellow Corn Tortillas, 6 inch size
1 qt.	Meatless Chili, recipe on page 140
1 qt.	Enchilada Sauce, recipe on page 190
2 oz.	Soy Fat Free Cheddar Cheese, shredded
2 oz.	Soy Fat Free Monterey Jack with Jalapenos Cheese, shredded
1/4 cup	Black Olives (Optional)
1/2 cup	Guacamole (Optional)
1/2 cup	Soy or Rice Sour Cream (Optional)

Directions

1. Preheat oven to 400 degrees.
2. In a casserole dish ladle enough of the enchilada sauce in the bottom to coat.
3. Place the tortillas slightly overlapping over the sauce, and cover with the chili mix.
4. Cover the chili with more tortillas overlapping again, and cover with the refried bean.
5. Cover the beans with the tortillas, then coat with the enchilada sauce.
6. Sprinkle the cheese over and bake uncovered for about 30 minutes, until melted.
7. Remove and let rest for 5 minutes, cut and garnish with black olives and guacamole or soy sour cream.

Serves 6 - 8

Vegetable Quesadillas

This Mexican version of a grilled cheese sandwich can be made in just minutes.

1 ts.	Canola Oil or 1/4 cup of Water or Broth
3 each	Scallions, sliced 1/4 inch
1 ts.	Minced Garlic
8 oz.	Mushrooms, sliced
1 each	Zucchini, sliced lengthwise in half, then sliced in 1/4 inch thick slices
1 each	Yellow Squash, sliced the same as Zucchini
8 oz.	Fat Free Soy Cheddar Cheese
4 oz.	Fat Free Monterey Jack with Jalapeno Soy Cheese
6 each	Whole-Wheat Tortillas or Chapatis (they are softer in texture)
1 cup	Mexican Salsa, recipe on page 195

Directions

1. Heat oil to saute and add scallions, garlic and mushrooms.
2. Add the other vegetables, cover and steam for 3 - 5 minutes until tender.
3. Place the cooked vegetables in a strainer. Begin shredding the cheeses.
4. Place the tortillas on a flat surface and sprinkle the cheese evenly over half of the tortilla.
5. Spread 1/6 of the vegetable mix evenly over the cheese, sprinkle with more cheese and fold the empty side over to be half-moon shape.
6. Heat a teflon pan to medium high heat, brush lightly with canola oil. Place a tortilla in the pan and cook until lightly browned on one side and repeat quickly on the other side.
7. When the cheese has melted, but is not too runny, remove and place on a cutting board.
8. Begin cooking the remaining tortillas. Allow to cool slightly before cutting into pie-shaped wedges and serve warm.

Serves 4 - 6

Serve with Mexican salsa, guacamole and/or soy sour cream. At home when time is a factor, we like to eliminate the vegetables and make a cheese quesadilla for an easy meal after a long day.

Ratatouille

*This French vegetable stew is great with a whole wheat baguette
or served over brown rice.*

1 each	Small Eggplant, peeled and cut into 1 inch cubes
2 each	Zucchini, cut off ends, split down the middle and cut into 1 inch cubes
2 each	Yellow Squash, cut the same as Zucchini
2 each	Yellow Onions, peeled and cut into 1 inch cubes
2 each	Red Peppers, seeded and cut into 1 inch cubes
2 each	Yellow Peppers, seeded and cut into 1 inch cubes
8 oz.	Domestic or Shitakes Mushrooms, cut in half, if using Shitakes, discard the stems
2 tb.	Minced Garlic
1 tb.	Organic Olive Oil or 1/4 cup of Water or Broth
4 each	Large Vine Ripe Tomatoes, cored and diced into 1 inch cubes
1 can	Muir Glen Organic Tomato Puree
2 tb.	Fresh Chopped Oregano, or dry leaves will be fine
1 bunch	Fresh Chopped Basil
1 tb.	Thyme Leaves
2 each	Bay Leaves
1/2 ts.	Sea Salt, optional
dash	Cayenne Pepper

Directions

*First of all do not be misled by the long list of ingredients. Once you prep all
of your vegetables, the actual preparation is very enjoyable to complete.*

1. Rinse and cut all vegetables and herbs and set aside.
2. In a large pot heat the olive oil and saute the onions and garlic to a golden brown.
3. Add the peppers, eggplant and squash and continue cooking.
4. Add the tomato products and mushrooms and continue cooking.
5. Add the remaining herbs and spices, cover and simmer for about 45 minutes.
6. Adjust seasonings as necessary and stir on occasion.
   If time allows *(for better flavor)*, try roasting the peppers first.

Serves 4 - 6

Refried Beans

This versatile dish can be used as Hummus, for filling in Mexican Lasagne, in Burritos over Nacho Chips, in a 5-layer dip, and I am sure you can create a few more.

2 1/2 qts.	Distilled Water
1 lb.	Organic Kidney Beans, soaked in scalding water for 1-2 hours, then strain
2 each	Bay Leaves
2 tb.	Minced Garlic
1 each	Vidalia or Yellow Onion, diced 1/2 inch
1 each	Red Pepper, diced 1/2 inch
1 each	Yellow or Orange pepper, diced 1/2 inch
2 tb.	Ground Cumin
1/8 ts.	Cayenne Pepper
2 ts.	Sea Salt, optional

Directions

1. In a large pot bring the distilled water to a boil, strain the beans and add to the pot.
2. Add the bay leaves and garlic and boil for 1 hour.
3. Add all the remaining ingredients and cook for 1 hour or until beans are tender.
4. Adjust seasonings to your personal taste and while still hot puree the beans in a blender or food processor with some of the cooking liquid, until creamy in texture.

Yield is about 1 1/2 quarts

To save time you may use canned kidney beans and season and prepare as above. You can also substitute other bean varieties such as pinto or black beans.

Stuffed Peppers with Millet

This African grain provides a wonderful texture and is a protein-rich, healthy alternative to an old favorite. The millet can be pan or oven roasted before using for a nuttier flavor.

1 qt.	Distilled Water
2 cups	Organic Millet, rinse in a strainer with cool water
1 each	Bay Leaf
1 ts.	Sea Salt (Optional)
1/8 ts.	Cayenne Pepper
1 tb.	Organic Olive Oil or 1/4 cup of Water or Broth
1 each	Medium Yellow Onion, diced 1/2 inch
1 tb.	Minced Garlic
1 each	Small Zucchini or Summer Squash, diced 1/2 inch
1 bag	Fresh Spinach, cleaned and torn or 1 cup frozen chopped spinach, drained
1 cup	Frozen Baby Peas (Optional)
1 ts.	Thyme Leaves
2 each	Yellow or Orange Peppers rinsed, cut in half lengthwise and seeded, leave stem attached
2 each	Red Peppers, prepare the same as yellow peppers
3 ounces	Fat Free Soy Cheddar Cheese or other variety, shredded
1 qt.	Marinara Sauce or other tomato sauce

Directions

1. Bring water to a boil, add millet and next 3 spices. Cook for 20 minutes until water is absorbed and set aside to cool.
2. Preheat oven to 350 degrees.
3. Heat the olive oil and lightly saute the onions, garlic and squash.
4. Place millet in a large mixing bowl and mix in the cooked vegetables, herbs, peas and spinach.
5. Stuff the peppers with the millet mix and place in casserole dish lined with marinara sauce.
6. Spoon the marinara sauce over the stuffed peppers and top with cheddar cheese.
7. Bake uncovered for 45 minutes to an hour or until the peppers are tender and the cheese browned slightly.

Serves 6 - 8

Mock Scallops St. Jacques

This rendition of the classic Coquilles St. Jacques allows for the sea scallops to be replaced by hearts of palm. The similarities to the original dish are amazing. However, this sauce is made without Hollandaise Sauce, alcohol or heavy cream.

1 cup	De-alcoholized White Wine
1 each	Large Vidalia or Yellow Onion, diced 1/2 inch
2 ts.	Minced Garlic
8 oz.	Mushrooms, cut into 1/2 inch slices
1 each	Red Pepper, diced 1/2 inch
2 cans	Hearts of Palm, drain and slice into 1/2 inch thick cylinders

If you are fortunate to obtain fresh hearts of palm, they will be superior in texture and flavor.

1 box	Extra Firm, Silken Tofu, low fat if available
2 cups	Soy or Rice Milk
2 oz.	Soy Parmesan Cheese
1/4 cup	Black Olives slices, optional

Directions

1. In a large pan simmer the first 5 ingredients until tender, then add the hearts of palm.
2. In a blender puree the tofu and soy milk until creamy.
3. Fold into the vegetables the cream sauce, parmesan cheese and olives. Adjust spices as desired and turn off when heated. Be careful not to boil or the sauce may separate.
4. Preheat oven to broil at 500 degrees.
5. With a slotted spoon, place the vegetable mixture into a casserole dish or into individual scallop or coquille shells. Dust the top with parmesan cheese and gratinee on the top oven rack for about 30-45 seconds or until golden brown.

Serve hot over brown rice, your favorite pasta or, for a more traditional presentation, serve inside a border of garlic mashed potatoes that have been placed around the perimeter of the coquille shell or the casserole dish and gratinee as described above.

Serves 4 - 6

Crispy Tempeh

If you are not familiar with Tempeh, it is a fermented soybean cake. It can be found in a variety of different flavors and grains. The tempeh culture is formed into loaf shapes and can be cut into cubes or slices. Tempeh is extremely high in protein.

8 oz. pkg.	Tempeh (5 Grain, Wild Rice or other variety)
4 oz.	Bragg Liquid Aminos
4 oz.	Distilled Water
1/2 ts.	Minced Garlic
1/4 ts.	Minced Ginger
1/2 ts.	Liquid Hickory Smoke, optional for a more "bacon-like" aroma

Directions

1. Preheat oven to 400 degrees.
2. Slice Tempeh into 1/8 in slices.
3. In a blender puree Bragg, water and spices.
4. Add sliced Tempeh to the mixture and marinate for about 20 minutes.
5. Drain Tempeh into a colander.
6. Lightly rub a sheet pan with canola oil on a paper towel.
7. Place Tempeh on the pan and bake for about 30 minutes until brown on 1 side.
8. Remove from oven, flip the Tempeh over with a spatula and return to oven.
9. Bake about 15 minutes or until brown and crispy.

Serves 3 - 4

Serve with Pita Bread and your favorite salad items, crumbled on a tossed salad or baked potato, or add to enchance a Pasta Primavera salad.

Chinese Vegetable Spring Roll

*This lower fat version is made with phyllo pastry and is oven-baked
instead of deep-fried.*

1 qt.	Pure or Distilled Water
1/3 pkg.	Rice Noodles, available at Oriental or most health food stores
2 each	Carrots, cut lengthwise in half, and slice on the bias in 1/8 inch slices
2 stalks	Celery, slice in 1/8 inch slices
2 stalks	Bok Choy, trim and discard outer green leaves and slice into 1/8 inch slices
1 each	Medium Yellow Onion, cut in half and slice thinly
1 cup	Snow Peas, remove stem and cut on the bias in 3/4 inch slices
1 bunch	Scallions, slice into 1/4 inch slices
1 lb.	Bean Sprouts
1 tb.	Minced Garlic
1 tb.	Grated fresh Ginger
1/2 cup	Tamari, Shoyu or Soy Sauce - use the low-sodium varieties
1 ts.	5 Spice Powder, available in Oriental markets and some health food stores
1 cup	Pure or Distilled Water
1 pkg.	Phyllo Pastry, available in the frozen baked section of most supermarkets
1/2 cup	Canola or Peanut Oil

Vegetable Spring Roll *(continued)*
Directions

1. Bring the first listed water to boil and cook the rice noodles 3-4 minutes, then strain and shock with cool running water.
2. While the water is heating for the rice noodles, begin preparing all vegetables.
3. Bring the garlic, ginger, tamari and 2nd water to a boil in a wok or wide pan.
4. Add all the vegetables to the stock, cover, bring to a boil, then simmer for 2 minutes.
5. Place the vegetables into a strainer with a bowl below the strainer to reserve the liquid and allow to cool.
6. Toss the vegetables, 5 spice powder and rice noodles with about 1/4 cup of the stock.
7. Preheat the oven to 400 degrees.
8. On a clean dry table lay 2 pieces of phyllo pastry. Brush the canola oil lightly over the phyllo, then fold the phyllo in half lenghtwise and brush lightly again with the oil.
9. With a slotted spoon place 1 cup of vegetable noodle mix along the center of the phyllo leaving empty about 1 1/2 inches on each side so you can fold the pastry under. The amount of vegetables you place in the phyllo will determine how thick the roll will be.
10. Roll the phyllo and vegetables tightly and tuck the outer edges of the pastry on the underside of the roll. Place the roll on an oiled sheet pan and brush the outside of the pastry lightly with the canola oil.
    Repeat steps 8 through 10 with the remaining vegetables and phyllo.
11. Place on the bottom rack of the oven and bake for 20 minutes or until the pastry is golden.

Remove from the pan with a metal spatula, cut in half and serve with Mango Duck Sauce, recipe on page 193 or other Oriental dipping sauces.

Makes 4 -6 spring rolls

Wild Mushroom Dressing

This hearty dressing is a holiday favorite.
Serve it with Turkey-Style Tofu and Savory Gravy.

1 ts.	Canola Oil or 1/4 cup of Water or Broth
1 each	Large Yellow Onion, diced 1/2 inch
1 ts.	Minced Garlic
3 each	Portabella Mushrooms, with a spoon scoop out the gills on the underside of the cap or 8 oz. Shitake Mushrooms, destemmed and sliced
8 slices	Whole Wheat Bread, cut into 1 inch cubes
2 ts.	Sage
1 cup	Savory Gravy, recipe on page 199

Directions

1. Heat the oil to saute the onions and garlic until lightly brown.
2. Add the mushrooms, cover and cook until tender.
3. Strain most of the liquid off the mushrooms and toss the mushrooms with the wheat bread cubes and sage.
4. Fold in some of the Savory gravy and all of the vegetables from the gravy until bread is moist.
5. Preheat the oven to 375 degrees, place the dressing in a casserole and bake 30 - 40 minutes until crispy.

Serves 4

Vegetables

Clockwise from top left: Portabella Mushroom Burger, Vegetable Lasagne and Pasta with Pesto Sauce, Wild Mushrooms and Sundried Tomatoes. Now that we are eating more vegetables, consider buying organic produce to avoid the dangerous pesticides.

Asparagus
with Roasted Pine Nuts

Asparagus is now available year round thanks to modern technology, so why wait for February! Contrary to popular belief, the larger asparagus can be just as tender as the thin asparagus. We must use caution and only cook the asparagus until just tender. Serve immediately or cool down and reheat right before service.

2 bunches	Medium Asparagus
1 cup	Pure or Distilled Water
1/4 cup	Fresh Lemon Juice, 3 lemons approximately
1 cup	Pine Nuts

Directions

1. Preheat oven to 400 degrees and place the water in a large saute pan until boiling.
2. Place the pine nuts on a sheet pan and bake 12-15 minutes or until browned lightly.
3. Add the asparagus to the saute pan, cover and steam 3-5 minutes until just tender.
4. Remove asparagus, place in a casserole and drizzle over the lemon juice.
5. Sprinkle the roasted pine nuts over the asparagus and serve immediately.

Serves 4 - 6

Feel free to try other toasted nuts, such as almond slivers or slices, cashews or Macademia nuts. Roasted Red Pepper Sauce is also a nice accompaniment.

Broccoli
with Garlic, Coconut and Tamari Sauce

The tantalizing flavors of the Tamari sauce
will give steamed broccoli a new dimension.

1 head	Broccoli, cut into spears and remove outer leaves
1/2 cup	Low Sodium Tamari
1/3 cup	Unsweetened Coconut Flakes

(If using sweetened coconut, try the sauce before adding the Rice Syrup)

1/4 cup	Brown Rice Syrup
1/4 cup	Distilled or Pure Water
2 ts.	Minced Garlic
dash	Cayenne Pepper

Directions

1. Steam or boil the broccoli 8-10 minutes until just tender.
2. While the broccoli is cooking, place remaining ingredients in a blender and puree.
3. Drain broccoli, brush the sauce lightly over and serve hot.

Serves 3 - 4

Stir-Steamed Brussels Sprouts

Brussels sprouts have as many lovers as detractors,
this recipe may appeal to both.

1 pint	Brussels Sprouts, trimmed and cut in half
2 each	Carrots, peeled if not organic and sliced diagonally in 1/4 inch slcies
3 each	Scallions, cut in 1/2 inch slices
1 each	Red or Yellow Pepper, seeded and cut into 1 inch squares
1/4 cup	Pure or Distilled Water
2 tb.	Low-Sodium Tamari or Soy Sauce
1 ts.	Minced Garlic
1 ts.	Freshly ground Ginger

Directions

1. Cook or steam Brussels sprouts 10-12 minutes or until tender, then drain and set aside.
2. In a large saute pan or wok, add the water, garlic, ginger and tamari and bring to a boil.
3. Add the carrots, scallions and peppers, cover and steam 2-3 minutes.
4. Add the Brussels sprouts, toss and serve hot.

Serves 4 - 6

Beets à l'Orange

*Red Beets fall into the same category of appreciation as Brussels sprouts.
It is only fair that we provide beet lovers with a recipe as well.*

2 qts.	Pure or Distilled Water
2 lbs.	Fresh Beets, peeled, halved and sliced 1/2 inch thick
2 tb.	Orange Rind, grated
2 cups	Fresh Sqeezed Orange Juice
1/2 cup	Brown Rice Syrup or 2 tb. Sucanat
1 ts.	Fresh Ground Ginger or 1/2 ts. of powdered ginger
1/4 cup	Pure or Distilled Water
3 tb.	Arrowroot

Directions

1. Bring a pot of water to a boil and cook the beets 18-20 minutes or until tender.
2. In a separate sauce pot add the next 4 ingredients and bring to a boil.
3. Dissolve the water and arrowroot and whip into the orange juice mixture until slightly thickened.
4. Add the cooked beets, cover and simmer, adjust flavorings as desired and serve.

Serves 4 - 6

Cumin Spiced Cabbage

While steamed cabbage itself is very tasty and pleasing to the stomach, this spicy version provides a nice change for cabbage lovers. Steamed cabbage with stewed tomatoes, recipe on page 196 is another way to enjoy green cabbage.

1 head	Small Green Cabbage, cored and sliced 1/2 inch
1 cup	Pure or Distilled Water
2 tb.	Apple Cider Vinegar
2 tb.	Bragg Liquid Aminos
1 ts.	Ground Cumin or Cumin Seeds
1 ts.	Chili Powder

Directions

1. In a large pot steam the water and cabbage, covered, until just tender.
2. Add the Bragg and spices, toss and serve hot.

Serves 4 - 6

Carrot Tsimmes

This traditional Jewish holiday vegetable is loved by all nationalities.

6 each	Organic Carrots, scrubbed and sliced into 1/2 inch slices
1 cup	Fresh Orange Juice
1 ts.	Grated Orange Rind, you may grate the orange before squeezing for juice
1/2 cup	Brown Rice Syrup or Honey
1/2 ts.	Cinnamon
1/4 ts.	Ground Nutmeg
1/3 cup	Arrowroot, dissolve in about 1/4 cup of cool water
1 cup	Pineapple Chunks, cut into 1 inch squares
2/3 cup	Pitted Prunes or Raisins

Directions

1. Steam the carrots until tender, drain and set aside
2. While carrots are cooking bring orange juice, rind, syrup and spice to a boil.
3. Slowly whip in the arrowroot mix until thickened.
4. Add the prunes, pineapple and carrots, simmer for 10-15 minutes and serve hot.

Serves 4 - 6

Tangy Carrots

If you are looking to liven up your steamed carrots,
look no further than the recipe below.

6 each   Organic Carrots if available, scrubbed and sliced
              1/4 inch thick on the bias
1/2 cup   Wildflower Honey or Brown Rice Syrup
1/3 cup   Fresh squeezed Lime Juice
2 ts.   Fresh grated Ginger

Directions

1.   Boil or steam carrots 6 - 8 minutes until just tender.
2.   Puree the next 3 ingredients in a blender.
3.   Heat the lime honey sauce and add the carrots, toss and serve
      hot.

Serves 4

For additional variety you can try this recipe with turnips, parsnips, jicama,
fresh beets, or any combination of these vegetables.

Creamy Cauliflower and Baby Peas

*The use of soy sour cream in this recipe
provides a wonderful non-dairy alternative.*

1 head	Cauliflower, cut into florettes
10 oz.pkg.	Frozen Baby Peas, thawed
1 1/2 cups	Soy Sour Cream or Rice Sour Cream
2 tb.	Bragg Liquid Aminos
2 ts.	Minced Garlic
dash	Cayenne Pepper
2 tb.	Chopped Fresh Dill

Directions

1. Steam or cook the cauliflower florettes for 8-10 minutes or until just tender.
2. In a large pot add the soy sour cream, garlic, Bragg and pepper and simmer.
3. When the sour cream mix is hot, toss with the cauliflower, peas and dill.
4. Adjust spices as needed and serve hot.

Serves 4 - 6

Baked Cho - Chos
(Chayote Squash)

*The Chayote Squash has been a favorite for years in
Central America and the Caribbean.
It is light green in color, and its shape and texture are somewhat like a pear.*

1 quart	Distilled or Pure Water
2 each	Chayote Squash, peeled, halved and remove seed

Topping

1 cup	Whole-Wheat Bread Crumbs
1 tb.	Fresh chopped Parsley
2 ts.	Chopped Basil Leaves
1 tb.	Organic Cold Pressed Olive Oil
1 ts.	Minced Garlic
2 tb.	Lite Soy Parmesan Cheese or shredded Fat Free Soy Cheddar Cheese
dash	Cayenne Pepper
1/4 ts.	Sea Salt (Optional)

Directions

1. Bring water to a boil add the squash and cook or steam for 10-15 minutes or until tender.
2. Preheat oven to 400 degrees.
3. Drain the squash and cool, meanwhile toss the remaining ingredients in a bowl.
4. Place squash with seeded side facing upwards on a sheet pan.
5. Lightly pack about 2-3 tablespoons of topping evenly covering the entire squash.
6. Bake 15-20 minutes on the top rack until golden brown and crispy and serve hot.

Serves 4

Cajun Corn and Okra

This vegetable can be served hot or as a salad
for a New Orleans Style Brunch.

2 cups	Fresh or frozen cut Corn
1 lb.	Fresh Okra, wash and cut off stems (frozen can be used but fresh is preferred)
2 cups	Stewed Tomatoes, recipe on page 198
2 ts.	Cajun Spice, use a low-sodium spice

Directions

1. Steam okra and corn about 10 minutes or until the okra is tender and drain.
2. Add the steamed vegetables to the stewed tomatoes, adjust spices and serve.

Serves 4 - 6

Grilled Eggplant
with Roasted Peppers

This dish is wonderful as a hot vegetable or chilled as an appetizer salad.

1/4 cup	Pure or Distilled Water
2 tb.	Olive Oil
1 tb.	Fresh chopped Basil or Oregano
1 ts.	Fresh minced Garlic
2 tb.	Bragg Liquid Amino Acids
dash	Cayenne Pepper
1 each	Eggplant, organic if available, rinse and cut with skin on into 1/2 inch thick slices
2 each	Red, Orange or Yellow Peppers, cut into quarters and discard seeds

Directions

1. Place first 6 ingredients in a blender and puree or whip rapidly by hand to incorporate.
2. Place sliced eggplant into casserole and add the marinade. Turn occasionally, while marinating for 1-2 hours.
3. Preheat grill to the high setting while the eggplant is marinating.
4. Place the eggplant on the hot grill, when dark grill marks appear, flip over and repeat.
5. At the same time, grill the peppers skin side down, until the skin is charred. Remove and when cooled peel the skin away and discard the skin.
6. Place eggplant overlapping on a bed of lettuce and garnish with the roasted peppers.

Changes are that it is difficult to grill in February in Chicago. You can set your oven to broil - 500 degrees and place the vegetables on a sheet pan. Broil on the top oven rack with similar results.

Serves 3 - 4

Green Beans Lyonnaise

You will be amazed at how caramelizing the onions eliminates any need for salt or spices.

2 qts.	Distilled or Pure Water
1 lb.	Fresh Green Beans, Wax Beans, Haricots Vertes or Sugar Snap Peas, cut the stems and rinse
1 ts.	Canola or Peanut Oil
2 each	Vidalia Onions or other, peeled, cut in half and slice 1/2 inch thick
1 ts.	Minced Fresh Garlic, optional

Directions

1. Bring water to a boil, add beans and cook about 10 minutes or until tender.
2. Pour the beans into a strainer and set aside.
3. In a large saute pan add the oil and heat very hot.
4. Add the sliced onions (do not stir the onions for up to 1-2 minutes, this will allow them to brown). You may now stir the onions, but after stirring let the onions saute once again resisting the temptation to stir them. It is this caramelizing that will give the onions their wonderful flavor. You can now add the garlic if desired.
5. Now add the beans and toss. Serve when the beans are hot.

Serves 4 - 6

For additional variety, try oven-roasted pine nuts or toasted sesame seeds for garnish, and replace the beans with asparagus or zucchini.

Grilled Vegetable Kabobs

If you are looking for exciting ways to use your freshly harvested squash and peppers and you need another reason to fire up the grill, this recipe should satisfy both desires.

1/4 cup	Fresh Lemon Juice
1/2 cup	Olive Oil
1 tb.	Fresh chopped Basil, Oregano or Tarragon
1 ts.	Fresh minced Garlic
1/2 ts.	Sea Salt, optional
dash	Cayenne Pepper
1 each	Yellow Squash, cut into 1 inch cubes
1 each	Zucchini, cut into 1 inch cubes
1 each	Vidalia or Yellow Onion, cut in half, then cut into 1 inch cubes, 2-3 layers thick
1 each	Red or Orange Peppers, cut into 1 inch squares
16 each	Medium Mushrooms, cut off the stem, do not remove the inner stem in the cap
8 each	6 inch wooden skewers, larger skewers are OK to use

Directions

1. Place first 6 ingredients in a blender and puree or whip rapidly by hand to incorporate.
2. Cut all vegetables, being sure to cut in the same size for uniform cooking.
3. Assemble the kabobs by alternating the squash, onions and peppers from end to end.
4. Place the mushroom caps at each end of the skewers.
5. Preheat the grill to the high setting while preparing the kabobs. *You may also use the oven broiler set at 500 degrees.*
6. Brush the marinade over the vegetables. Turn over and brush again.
7. Place the kabobs on the hot grill, when dark grill marks appear , flip over and brush with some of the marinade for added flavor.

Serves 4, two skewers per person

Serve on a bed of brown rice or pasta with Roasted Red Pepper Sauce, Salsa Verde, Spicy Thai Peanut Sauce, Sundried Tomato Tapenade or Cilantro Aioli Sauce. For variety try adding eggplant cubes onto the kabobs.

Roasted Peppers

Roasting brings out the natural sweetness of bell peppers and imparts a slightly smoky taste. It is much easier than you think to prepare. We do not recommend using raw green peppers in our recipes due to the fact that they are an unripened pepper! However, roasted green peppers are acceptable.

3 each	Red, Yellow, Orange or Green Peppers
1 ts.	Canola or Peanut Oil

Directions

1. Preheat oven on the broil setting and 500 degrees.
2. Slice the peppers in a way that will keep the pepper in flat 2 inch wide slices.
3. Oil a sheet pan lightly with a paper towel and place the peppers skin side up.
4. Place the pan on the top rack of the preheated oven and roast until slightly charred, for approximately 15-18 minutes and remove.
5. Cover the pan with another inverted pan and let steam for about 5 minutes.
   You may also enclose the peppers in a plastic bag and steam for 5 minutes.
6. When cooled, the charred skin is to be removed. Serve the peppers as is, julienned or chopped as a garnish or complement to your favorite salads, vegetables or entrees.

Serves 4

You may also try roasting the peppers skin side down on the grill or over an open flame while holding with a pair of metal tongs until the skin is charred.

171

Orange & Ginger Glazed Plantains

Plantains, shaped like an over-sized banana, are a mainstay of the Caribbean Cuisine! When yellow and firm they are served by actually being pan-fried, then mashed down and pan-fried again. Hardly a low-fat preparation. Another way to enjoy plantains is to let them over-ripen and actually have the skin turn black before using. This is how we will use them for this recipe.

2 each	Very ripe Plantains, peeled and cut lengthwise in half, then cut in quarters
1 cup	Fresh Sqeezed Orange Juice
2/3 cup	Brown Rice Syrup or Wildflower Honey
1 tb.	Fresh Ground Ginger
1 tb.	Sesame Seeds

Directions

1. In a sauce pot combine the juice, syrup and ginger, bring to a rolling boil and reduce to half of its original volume.
2. Preheat oven to 400 degrees.
3. Place the sliced plantains flat side down on a casserole dish or baking sheet.
4. Drizzle the syrup over the plantains, then sprinkle the sesame seeds over.
5. Bake for 20-25 minutes or until the sesame seeds are light brown and serve hot with remaining syrup.

Serves 3 - 4

Italian Spinach Saute

This wonderful hot vegetable, if not overcooked,
is also a great salad when chilled.

1/2 cup	Pine Nuts, roasted on a sheet pan
2 pkg.	Fresh Spinach, remove stems and wash thoroughly
2 ts.	Organic Cold Pressed Olive Oil
6 each	Fresh Garlic Cloves, peel and slice thinly
1 each	Vidalia Onion, peeled, halved and sliced 1/2 inch
1/2 ts.	Sea Salt, Optional
1/4 ts.	Ground Nutmeg
dash	Cayenne Pepper

Directions

1. Preheat oven to 400 degrees and roast the pine nuts 12-15 minutes or until golden brown.
2. While the pine nuts are roasting, clean and cut the vegetables.
3. Heat a saute pan, add oil and saute the onions and garlic until lightly browned.
4. Add the spinach and spices, cover and simmer until the spinach is just tender.
5. Strain off the liquid from the spinach, add the pine nuts, toss and serve.

Serves 4

For a flavorful addition, try adding one cup of fresh julienne fennel to the
sauteed onions and proceed with the recipe.

Spanokopitas

This classic Greek specialty is rekindled with soy mozzarella replacing the feta cheese. You may also add crumbled tofu.

2 lb.	Frozen Chopped Spinach, thawed and pressed dry in a strainer, fresh spinach is great, but more labor intensive.
2 ts.	Canola Oil or Olive Oil
2 each	Vidalia or Yellow Onion, diced 1/2 inch
2 ts.	Minced Garlic
1/8 ts.	Cayenne Pepper
1/2 ts.	Nutmeg
8 oz.	Soy Mozzarella Cheese, shredded or cubed
1/3 cup	Canola or Peanut Oil
1 pkg.	Phyllo pastry, "Athens" is a recognizable brand name

Directions

1. Preheat oven to 375 degrees.
2. Lightly brown the onions and garlic in canola oil.
3. In a mixing bowl toss the spinach, spices and mozzarella together.
4. Brush the bottom of a 9 x 13 casserole lightly with the second canola oil.
5. Layer 2 pieces of phyllo on bottom of pan and brush lightly with oil.

Pastry will be too large for the dish but you may precut it to come up the sides of pan.

Continued on next page.

Spanokopitas (continued)

6. Repeat step 5 with 2 more layers of pastry and brush lightly with oil again.
7. Spread spinach mixture evenly over the pastry, being sure to fill the corners.
8. At this point you can fold the excess phyllo back over the top of the spinach mix.
9. Cover the spinach with 2 layers of phyllo tucking it into the sides and corners of the pan with the pastry brush and brush lightly with oil.
10. Place two more layers of pastry using the same procedures as above.

For easier serving pre-cut the pastry into squares before baking. Now dip a pastry brush into water and brush along the just cut pastry lines. This will reduce some of the flakiness when serving.

A special thank you to Demetra Abdulla for this helpful hint.

11. Bake on the top oven rack for 20 - 25 minutes or until golden brown.
12. Remove from oven and serve with a sharp spatula.

If you do not serve when hot, the phyllo may soften. Simply return the casserole to the oven and reheat until crispy. If there are leftovers, remove from the refrigerator, bring to room tempeature and reheat at 375 degrees 12-15 minutes or until the pastry is crispy.

Serves 6 - 8

Hints: Phyllo pastry is very delicate to work with. Its biggest enemies are air and water. When not using, be sure to keep covered with a towel or plastic wrap. Keep your work area dry. If the pastry tears or is broken do not despair, just patch with more phyllo as necessary, but try to keep the top layer in one piece for a better presentation.

Summer Squash Sauté

This very colorful vegetable can be made fat-free
by replacing the olive oil with vegetable broth.

4 each	Yellow Squash, cut in half lengthwise, scoop out seeds and cut slice 1/2 inch
1 ts.	Extra Virgin Olive Oil
1 each	Vidalia Onion, peeled, cut in half and sliced in 1/4 inch slices
1 ts.	Fresh minced Garlic
1 each	Red Pepper, remove seeds and cut into 1 inch cubes
2 ts.	Fresh chopped Oregano
dash	Cayenne Pepper

Directions

1. Heat oil to saute, and lightly brown the onions and garlic.
2. Add the squash and peppers, cook on a medium high heat and toss in the spices.
3. Adjust spices as desired and serve hot.

Serves 4

Grilled Tomatoes with Aioli

Grilling tomatoes is more flavorful than the better known fried green tomatoes, and they become spectacular with this cilantro and garlic mayonnaise.

3 each	Large Green or Vine Ripe Tomatoes, cored and sliced in 3/4 inch thick slices
1 tb.	Canola or Peanut Oil
1/4 cup	Cold Pressed Olive Oil
1 tb.	Fresh Lemon Juice
1 ts.	Minced Garlic
1/2 bunch	Fresh Cilantro, destemmed and chop coarsely
1/4 ts.	Sea Salt
dash	Cayenne Pepper

Directions

1. Turn on barbecue to high setting. For a smokier flavor place soaked mesquite chips over the coals.
2. Lightly brush the canola oil over the sliced tomatoes and grill on both sides until hot.
3. Place the remaining ingredients in a blender and puree thoroughly, scraping down the sides of the blender as necessary.
4. Lightly drizzle a little of the aioli over the cooked tomatoes and serve.

Serves 4

Baked Tomatoes
"Provencale"

Once the topping is made this is a very easy gratinee vegetable to prepare.

3 each	Large Vine Ripe Tomatoes
1 1/2 cups	Whole Wheat Bread Crumbs
2 tb.	Grated Soy Parmesan Cheese or fat-free Soy Cheddar Cheese
1 1/2 ts.	Minced Garlic
2 tb.	Organic Olive Oil
2 tb.	Chopped Italian Parsley, Basil or Oregano leaves
dash	Cayenne Pepper

Directions

1. Preheat oven to 400 degrees.
2. Core the tomatoes, cut in half and place cut side up on a sheet pan.
3. In a small bowl mix the remaining ingredients.
4. In one hand hold the tomato and in the other hand place about 1/4 inch of the bread crumb topping on the tomato, covering completely.
5. Return the tomatoes to the sheet pan and bake on the top rack of the oven for about 15 minutes or until the bread crumbs are brown and crispy. Do not over-bake because the tomatoes have a tendency to split open from the extreme heat.

Serves 4 - 6

If any bread crumb mix is leftover, it can be refrigerated for future uses.

Grilled Vegetables

The Bar-B-Que grill plays a great role in our cuisine.
It will truly liven up your meals.

These vegetables are excellent for grilling. I am sure you will discover others:
Eggplant, Zucchini, Summer Squash, Sweet or Idaho Potatoes, Green Tomatoes,
Tomatillos, Portabella or Shitake Mushrooms, Red, Orange or Yellow Peppers.

Marinade

1/2 cup	Canola, Peanut or Olive Oil
1 each	Red or Yellow Pepper, cut in cubes
1 tb.	Fresh chopped herbs... basil, oregano, tarragon, thyme, rosemary etc., or any combination of your favorite fresh herbs. Dry herbs will do in a pinch.
1 ts.	Fresh minced Garlic
1/4 ts.	Sea Salt (Optional) or 1 tb. Bragg Liquid Aminos
dash	Cayenne Pepper

Place all ingredients in a blender and puree thoroughly.

Directions

1. Preheat the grill to the high setting while preparing the vegetables.
2. Rinse and slice your favorite vegetables into 1/2 inch slices. If you are using peppers, clean and cut down the side of the pepper to lay flat. To grill mushrooms, destem and clean.
3. Arrange the vegetables on a sheet pan and brush lightly with the marinade.
4. Place the brushed side of the vegetables on the grill rack and then brush the top side of the vegetables while they are grilling.
5. When dark grill marks appear on the bottom side flip over the vegetables and repeat.
6. Serve hot or, if you would like the vegetables to be more tender, place in a 375 degree oven to finish.

For added flavor sensations place some water-soaked mesquite or hickory chips over the grill stones before using.

Winter Squash and Apple Gratin

This is a nice casserole for those chilly fall and winter days.

1 ts.	Canola or Peanut Oil
1 each	Large Yellow or Vidalia Onion, peeled, cut in half and sliced into 1/2 inch slices
1 ts.	Minced Garlic
2 each	Butter Nut or Acorn Squash, peeled, seeded and sliced 1/2 inch slices
1/2 cup	Organic Apple Juice
2 each	Granny Smith Apples, peeled if not organic, seeded and sliced 1/2 inch
dash	Ground Nutmeg
1 1/2 cups	Whole Wheat Bread Crumbs
1 tb.	Light Olive Oil
1/3 cup	Fat Free Soy Cheddar Cheddar or Soy Parmesan Cheese
dash	Cayenne Pepper

Directions

1. Heat oil to saute, add onions, brown lightly, add garlic and toss.
2. Add squash and apple juice and continue to cook. Preheat oven to 400 degrees.
3. When squash is just just tender, add the apples and nutmeg, cover and simmer 3 minutes.
4. While the squash is cooking, in a small bowl toss the remaining ingredients.
5. Place the vegetables in a casserole, top with bread crumb mix and bake until crispy.

Serves 4 - 6

Zucchini
with Fines Herbes

For an Italian theme dinner, try this unique tasting side dish.

2 each	Zucchini, remove stem, cut in half lengthwise and cut into 1/2 inch slices
1 ts.	Extra Virgin Olive Oil
1 each	Vidalia Onion, peeled, cut in half and sliced 1/4 inch slices
1 ts.	Fresh minced Garlic
dash	Cayenne Pepper
2 ts.	Fresh chopped Basil or Oregano
3 tb.	Toasted Whole Wheat Bread Crumbs
3 tb.	Soy Parmesan Cheese, toss with bread crumbs

Directions

1. Heat oil to saute and lightly brown the onions and garlic.
2. Add the zucchini, continue to cook on a medium high heat and toss in the spices.
3. Preheat oven to 400 degrees. Place bread crumbs and soy cheese on a sheet pan and bake 15 - 18 minutes on the top rack until brown and crispy.
4. Serve hot and garnish with the toasted bread crumbs and soy parmesan cheese.

Serves 4

Okra with Stewed Tomatoes

This vegetable combination goes well with a "Cajun-Style" meal such as Jambalaya, grilled tofu steaks or any variety of rice and beans.

1 lb.	Fresh Okra, cut off stems and rinse
1 tb.	Organic Olive Oil
1 each	Large Vidalia Onion, diced 1/2 inch
1 each	Yellow Pepper, diced 1/2 inch
1 each	Red Pepper, diced 1/2 inch
1 tb.	Minced Garlic
2 cans	Muir Glen Organic Diced Tomatoes, or other
1 cup	Muir Glen Organic Tomato Puree, or other
6 oz.	Brown Rice Syrup or 3 tb. Sucanat
1/2 bunch	Fresh Basil, chopped
2 each	Bay Leaves
1/2 ts.	Sea Salt, optional
dash	Cayenne Pepper

Directions

1. Heat olive oil in a stainless steel sauce pot, add the onions, peppers and garlic and saute until tender.
2. Add the tomatoes, herbs and spices and simmer up to one hour while stirring frequently. Adjust seasonings as desired.
3. While the tomatoes are cooking, steam the okra about 8-10 minutes until just tender. Drain off the water from the okra.
4. Place the okra into a pot or casserole and fold in as much of the stewed tomatoes as desired. Allow okra about 10 minutes to absorb the flavors and serve hot as is or over brown rice pilaf.

Serves 4 - 6

Sauces

    The sauces in this book are free of butter, margarine and flour. They have been emulsified at times with silken tofu. All the sauces contain less than 1 gram of saturated fat per serving.

Alfredo Sauce

This sauce is very similar to the original Alfredo Sauce in flavor and texture, however, it is cholesterol-free and lower in fat calories. It can be used with your favorite pastas or you can interchange other fat-free soy cheeses in place of the soy parmesan cheese to create an au gratin sauce.

2 cups	Rice Dream or other Rice Milk
10 oz. box	Extra Firm or Firm Silken Tofu, low-fat, if available
1 ts.	Fresh minced Garlic
1/2 ts.	Sea Salt, optional
dash	Ground Nutmeg
dash	Cayenne Pepper or 1/4 ts. Ground Black Pepper
1 cup	Soy Parmesan Cheese, Lite n Less by Soyco or Soymage
2 ts.	Fresh chopped Basil or Parsley (Optional)

Directions

1. Place all ingredients except for the parsley and soy cheese in a blender and puree. Scrape down the sides of the blender and repeat.
2. Place blended items in a sauce pot and simmer until hot, stirring occasionally.
3. Whip in the soy parmesan cheese and basil, adjust seasonings as desired and serve hot.

Be careful not to boil the sauce, it may tend to separate.

Yield is 1 qt.

Basic Cream Sauce

This sauce can replace any of your favorite recipes involving dairy. Be careful not to let the sauce come to a boil, it may separate under intense heat. To correct a separated sauce, return to the blender and puree.

2 cups	Soy Milk or Rice Dream
10 oz. box	Extra Firm Silken Tofu
1/2 ts.	Sea Salt
dash	Ground Nutmeg
dash	Cayenne Pepper

Directions

1. Place all ingredients in a blender and puree.
2. Place blended items in a sauce pot and simmer until hot, stirring occasionally.

Yields 3 cups

This sauce can also be used as a base for cheese sauces. It can be infused with saffron threads, or flavored with other herbs and vegetables to create exciting new cream sauces.

Hickory Smoked Barbecue Sauce

Most barbecue sauces are sweetened with corn syrup or molasses, which have at least 80% natural sugar content. We use organic brown rice syrup as the sweetener. It has only 20% natural sugar content.

16 oz.	Organic Tomato Puree
1 cup	Brown Rice Syrup
1/4 cup	Vegetarian Worcestershire Sauce
1/4 cup	Apple Cider Vinegar
1 ts.	Minced Garlic
1 ts.	Liquid Smoke
1 ts.	Thai Red Chili Paste, available in the Oriental section of most stores, or any other of your favorite hot sauces.

Directions

1. In a sauce pot, simmer the tomato puree and brown rice syrup.
2. Dissolve the chili paste in a bowl with the remaining ingredients.
3. Fold chili paste mixture into the tomato sauce, simmer and stir from time to time.

Yield is 3 cups

This sauce can transform thinly sliced seitan (which is a wheat gluten product that resembles meat in texture) into a Bar-B-Q Beef style dish. Toss the sliced seitan with some of the sauce and serve hot or cold with a sliced scallion garnish. You can also use it on grilled tofu steaks, tempeh or veggie burgers.

Mock Bearnaise Sauce

This remake of the classic but unhealthy original version
is similar in color, flavor and texture.

1 cup	Soy Milk
4 tb.	Fresh Lemon Juice
2 ts.	Tarragon Leaves
1/4 ts.	Sea Salt
1 ts.	Tumeric
dash	Cayenne Pepper
2 tb.	Arrowroot
1/4 cup	Distilled or Pure Water

Directions

1. Combine the first 6 items in a sauce pot and bring to its scalding point.
2. Blend together the arrowroot and water and whip into the sauce until thickened.
3. Adjust seasonings to desired taste and hold covered. Reheat when needed.

Yield is 1 1/2 cups

• •

Stone Ground Mustard Sauce
with Basil

This unique condiment goes well with your favorite veggie burgers.

1/4 cup	Fresh Lemon Juice
1/2 cup	Stoneground Mustard
3 tb.	Brown Rice Syrup or Honey
2 tb.	Fresh chopped Basil

Directions

1. Combine all ingredients and puree in a blender.

Yield is 1 cup

Carrot Ginger Sauce

We use this sauce as an accompaniment for our Vegetable Sushi Rolls.

1/2 cup	Fresh Carrot Juice, from a juice extractor
2 tb.	Fresh Lemon Juice
1/4 cup	Distilled or Pure Water
2 ts.	Fresh Ginger, peeled and grated

Directions
Puree all ingredients in a blender and refrigerate until served.

Yield is 1 cup

• •

Chili Con Queso

This versatile fat-free sauce goes well as a dip for tortilla chips, or as a spicy cheese topping for a broccoli or cauliflower casserole.

1 each	Large Vine Ripe Tomato, diced 1/2 inch
4 each	Scallions, sliced 1/4 inch
1 each	Small Red Pepper, diced 1/4 inch
1 each	Jalapeno Pepper, finely chopped
1 tb.	Cilantro, finely chopped
8 oz.	Fat Free Soy Cheddar Cheese, shredded
2 ts.	Hot sauce, optional for a spicier flavor
1/4 ts.	Sea Salt, optional

Directions

1. In a sauce pot add the first 5 ingredients and simmer until vegetables are tender.
2. Stir in the soy cheeese until fully melted and adjust seasonings as desired.
3. Lower heat to warm and cover until served.

Yield is approximately 2 1/2 cups

Cilantro "Aioli" Sauce

This flavorful sauce can be used on toasted French bread slices or pita wedges.
It may also be used to flavor vegetables or as a garnish on bean soups.

1 bunch	Cilantro, rinsed, destemmed and chopped coarsely
1 ts.	Minced Garlic
1 tb.	Lemon Juice
1/4 ts.	Sea Salt
dash	Cayenne Pepper
1/3 cup	Organic Cold Pressed Olive Oil

Directions

Place all ingredients in a blender and puree thoroughly.
To prevent discoloring, cover sauce when not in use.

Yield is approximately 2/3 cup

This sauce will keep refrigerated for weeks,
but is best served at room temperature.

Enchilada Sauce

This spicy sauce, as the name suggests, can be served with any tortilla dish.

1 tb.	Organic Olive Oil
2 tb.	Minced Garlic
1 each	Vidalia or Yellow Onion, diced 1/2 inch
1 each	Red Pepper, diced 1/2 inch
1 each	Yellow or Orange pepper, diced 1/2 inch
16 oz.can	Organic Tomato Puree
3 tb.	Chili Powder
2 tb.	Cider Vinegar
1 tb.	Ground Cumin
1/8 ts.	Cayenne Pepper
1 ts.	Sea Salt, optional

Directions

1. In a sauce pan heat the olive oil and lightly brown the onions and garlic.
2. Add the peppers and continue to cook.
3. Add the remaining ingredients, adjusting spices to suit your taste.
4. Cover and simmer for about 30-40 minutes, stirring occasionally.

Yield is approximately 1 quart

Tropical Fruit Salsa

*This fat-free salsa often used on fish, can be used on grilled tofu steaks,
or as a colorful dip with blue corn tortilla chips.*

1 each	Mango, peeled and diced into 1/2 inch cubes
1 each	Papaya, peeled and diced into 1/2 inch cubes
1 cup	Diced Pineapple
1 each	Small Red or Yellow Pepper, cleaned and diced 1/2 inch
1 tb.	Finely chopped Cilantro
2 tb.	Fresh Lime Juice
1/4 cup	Brown Rice Syrup, if needed, depending on the ripeness of the fruit
1/2 ts.	Minced Jalapeno Pepper

Directions

Combine all ingredients in a non-reactive bowl.
Adjust spices as desired. Refrigerate until serving.

Yield is about 3 cups.

Salsa will keep for 3-4 days refrigerated.

Garlic, Tamari & Coconut Sauce

This sauce is so dynamic in its variety of flavors, I am sure you will find many uses. We use it to flavor steamed broccoli; it is also a wonderful dipping sauce for hors d'oeuvres and vegetables.

1/2 cup	Low Sodium Tamari
1/4 cup	Distilled Water
1/3 cup	Unsweetened Coconut Flakes

(If using sweetened coconut, try the sauce before adding the Rice Syrup)

1/4 cup	Brown Rice Syrup
1 tb.	Minced Garlic
dash	Cayenne Pepper

Directions

1. Place all ingredients in a blender and puree. Brush over steamed broccoli.

Yield 1 1/3 cups

This sauce will hold 2 weeks or more if refrigerated!

Mango Duck Sauce

Mangoes are now available year round. Choose ripe ones that are soft to touch.
Serve this spicy sauce with vegetable spring rolls or other Oriental favorites.

1 each	Large Mango, peeled and remove the flesh around the seed
1/4 each	Fresh Pineapple, peel, remove the core and cut into chunks
1/2 cup	Brown Rice Vinegar
2 tb.	Brown Rice Syrup
2 ts.	Fresh grated Ginger
2 ts.	Ume Plum Vinegar, available in Oriental and most health food stores
1/2 ts.	Thai Chili Paste, available in the Oriental section of most supermarkets

Directions

1. Place all ingredients in a blender and puree until smooth.

Yields approximately 1 1/2 cups

Marinara Sauce

This is my favorite Marinara recipe.
Organic tomatoes by Muir Glen definitely enhance this sauce.

2 tb.	Organic Olive Oil (Optional)
1 each	Large Yellow Onion, diced 1/2 inch
1 each	Yellow Pepper, diced 1/2 inch
1 each	Red Pepper, diced 1/2 inch
2 tb.	Minced Garlic
4 each	Vine Ripe Tomatoes, diced 3/4 inch or 24 oz. can Organic Diced Tomatoes
16 oz.	Muir Glen Organic Tomato Puree
2 tb.	Fresh Oregano, chopped fine
1 bunch	Fresh Basil, chopped fine
2 each	Bay Leaves
1/2 ts.	Crushed Red Pepper
1 ts.	Sea Salt, optional
1/3 cup	Brown Rice Syrup (may be added if the sauce is too acidic in flavor)

Directions

1. Heat olive oil in a heavy sauce pot. Add onions and garlic to brown slightly.
2. Add the peppers and continue to cook until tender.
3. Add remaining ingredients, reduce heat and simmer an hour or more, stirring frequently.
4. Adjust seasonings to your personal taste.

Yield is approximately 2 quarts

To reduce fat calories, steps 1 and 2 can be omitted. Place all ingredients in a large pot, cover and simmer. For additional variety and flavor you may add sliced domestic or wild mushrooms.

Mexican Salsa

This fat-free salsa, as most salsas are, can be used with Mexican entrees, for hors d'oeuvres or as a salad dressing.

4 each	Large Vine Ripe Tomatoes, cored and diced into 1/2 inch pieces
1 each	Vidalia or Red Onion, peeled, cored and diced 1/2 inch
1 each	Medium Yellow or Orange Pepper, diced 1/2 inch
1 each	Small Jalapeno Pepper, finely chopped without seeds
1 tb.	Organic Apple Cider Vinegar
1 bunch	Cilantro, rinsed and finely chopped
2 ts.	Minced Garlic
1/2 ts.	Sea Salt, optional

Directions

Combine all ingredients in a stainless steel bowl and chill before serving. Adjust spices as desired.

Yield is approximately 1 quart

For best quality use within 3 days. For a more intensely flavored salsa, try roasting the peppers first. Remove the charred skin and dice before adding.

Roasted Red Pepper Sauce

This brightly colored sauce is full of flavor and very versatile. It can be served to enhance steamed vegetables, grilled tofu steaks, lentil loaf, seafood or pasta.

3 each	Large Red Peppers, roasted and remove the charred skin
1 cup	Soy Milk or Rice Dream
4 oz.	Firm Silken Tofu, low-fat if available
1 ts.	Red Miso, available in Oriental or health food stores
1/2 ts.	Thai Chili Paste, can be found in most supermakets in the Oriental section
1 tb.	Fresh chopped Basil, optional

Directions

1. Roast peppers according to the recipe located in the vegetable chapter.
2. Place all ingredients except the basil in a blender and puree.
3. Remove sauce from the blender, place in a sauce pot with the basil and heat slowly. Do not boil or the sauce may separate.
4. When the sauce is hot adjust spices as desired and serve.
   If the sauce separates, return it to the blender and puree lightly.

Yield approximately 2 1/2 cups

For an artistic touch, place the sauce into a ketchup bottle and squirt around the outside of your entree plate or zig zag over the entree for a spectacular garnish.

This sauce will hold refrigerated for 5-7 days.

Salsa Verde

This colorful green mustard sauce is excellent over steamed vegetables or a legume loaf.

1 ts.	Canola Oil or Olive Oil
1 ts.	Minced Garlic
1 cup	Fresh chopped Spinach, packed tightly into the cup
1 tb.	Fresh chopped Cilantro or Parsley (Optional)
2/3 cup	Rice Dream or Soy Milk
1/4 ts.	Sea Salt, optional
dash	Nutmeg
dash	Cayenne Pepper
2 tb.	Stoneground Mustard
4 oz.	Firm Silken Tofu, low-fat variety

Directions

1. In a sauce pot heat the oil and saute the garlic, do not brown.
2. Add the spinach and cook until wilted. Do not overcook, the spinach may brown.
3. Add the non-dairy milk, and spices, and simmer until hot.
4. Place heated sauce and tofu in a blender and puree until well blended.
5. Adjust spices and thickness of the sauce as desired and serve hot or hold covered.

Yield is approximately 2 cups

To truly dazzle your guests, ladle a one ounce portion of this sauce and one ounce of the Roasted Red Pepper Sauce on opposite sides of an entree plate. Gently tilt the plate back and forth to "marry" the sauces together, being careful not to overlap them. Now place a grilled tofu steak, lentil loaf or other entree in the center of the plate for a memorable and tasty presentation.

Stewed Tomatoes

My mother Ann is the inspiration for this dish.
She would serve it over mashed potatoes or with steamed cabbage.

1 tb.	Organic Olive Oil
1 each	Large Yellow Onion, diced 1/2"
1 each	Yellow Pepper, diced 1/2"
1 each	Red Pepper, Diced 1/2 "
1 tb.	Minced Garlic
4 each	Vine Ripe Tomatoes, diced 3/4", or 16 oz. Organic Diced Tomatoes
2/3 cup	Muir Glen Organic Tomato Puree
6 oz.	Brown Rice Syrup
1/2 bunch	Fresh Basil, chopped fine
2 each	Bay Leaves
1/2 ts.	Sea Salt
dash	Cayenne Pepper

Directions

1. Heat olive oil in a heavy sauce pot. Saute onions, peppers and garlic.
2. When vegetables have softened, add all other ingredients. Simmer for an hour or more, stirring frequently.
3. Adjust seasonings to your personal taste.

If you would like to eliminate the fat calories of the oil, do not use it to saute. Simply place all ingredients, except for the oil, in a large pot and cook slowly.

Serves 3 - 4

Stewed Tomatoes are more nutritious when combined with fresh steamed okra, cabbage, green beans, Brussels sprouts or, like my mom does, with mashed potatoes.

Savory Gravy

This sauce goes well with bread dressings, "Turkey Style Tofu"
or mashed potatoes.

1 1/2 qts.	Water and Vegetable Broth base, Jensen's or Dr. Bonner's flavored to meet your tastes
2 tb.	Poultry Seasoning
1/8 ts.	Cayenne Pepper
2 each	Medium Yellow Onions, diced into 1/2 inch cubes
4 each	Celery Stalks, cut into 1/2 inch slices
2/3 cup	Arrowroot or Kuzu (Kuzu is used like arrowroot to thicken, but more costly)
1 cup	Cool Water

Directions

1. Bring broth to a boil and add all ingredients.
2. Cook until vegetables are tender and strain out the vegetables, reserving the broth into a sauce pot.
3. Return broth to a boil, dissolve the arrowroot in water and whip into broth until it reaches your desired thickness.
4. Return vegetables to the sauce, adjust seasonings and serve. Cover to avoid a skin forming on the top.

Yield approximately 1 3/4 quarts

For a heartier gravy add 8 oz. of sliced domestic or wild mushrooms.

Sundried Tomato Tapenade

*Spread over your favorite multi grain bread, pasta or vegetables
as a healthier alternative to butter.*

1/2 cup	Organic Olive Oil
1 1/2 ts.	Minced Garlic
1/2 bunch	Fresh chopped Basil
1/4 cup	Sundried Tomatoes, softened in hot water, and chopped coarsely
1/4 cup	Black Olives, pitted
1/8 tsp.	Sea Salt, optional

Directions

1. Place all ingredients in a blender or food processor and puree.

Yields 1 cup

*This sauce will hold for over 2 weeks once refrigerated.
To use again, return to room temperature before serving.*

Spicy Thai Peanut Sauce

*This sauce is excellent with vegetable kabobs, pasta,
grains or any Indonesian Sate dish.*

1 cup	Pure or Distilled Water
1/3 cup	Organic Peanut Butter, low-sodium if available
1 ts.	Minced Garlic
1 ts.	Yellow Miso
1/2 ts.	Thai Chili Paste or 1/8 ts. cayenne pepper

Directions

1. Simmer half of the water and the remaining ingredients in a sauce pan.
2. Whip in the remaining water until the sauce reaches the consistency desired.
3. Adjust seasonings and serve warm.

Yield is 1 1/2 cups

Pesto Sauce

This sauce is wonderful over salads, vegetables,
toasted whole grain breads or with your favorite pasta.

3/4 cup	Cold Pressed Extra Virgin Olive Oil
2 ts.	Minced Garlic
2 tb.	Chopped Walnuts or Pine Nuts
1/8 ts.	Sea Salt, optional
1/3 cup	Lite Soy Parmesan Cheese
1 bunch	Fresh Basil, chopped

Directions

Combine all ingredients in a blender and puree thoroughly.

This sauce can be refrigerated for up to a month.

Yield 12 ounces

For a more Tropical or Southwestern flare, replace the basil with cilantro.
Try replacing the basil with parsley for another flavor alternative.

Sundried Tomato Pesto Sauce

*Try this sauce with a salad of avocado and red onions
or with your favorite pasta.*

3/4 cup	Cold Pressed Extra Virgin Olive Oil
2 ts.	Minced Garlic
2 tb.	Chopped Walnuts or Pine Nuts
1/8 ts.	Sea Salt, optional
1/3 cup	Lite Soy Parmesan Cheese
1 bunch	Fresh Basil, chopped
1/2 cup	Sundried Tomatoes, softened in hot water, drained then chopped coarsely
dash	Cayenne Pepper

Directions

Combine all ingredients in a blender and puree thoroughly.

Yield 2 cups

*For a Southwestern Flair, replace the basil with cilantro
and a half teaspoon fresh jalapeno peppers.*

Pestos will hold well under refrigeration for at least 1 month.

Wild Mushroom Sauce

This versatile sauce can also be served as a soup.

1 ts.	Canola, Olive or Peanut Oil
1 each	Yellow Onion, 1/2 inch diced
1 ts.	Fresh minced Garlic
2 cups	Portabella, Shitake, Cremini, Trumpet or Morrels destemmed and sliced. You may substitute domestic Mushrooms
1/3 cup	Alcohol-Free White Wine or Balsamic Vinegar
1/3 cup	Chopped Sundried Tomatoes
1 cups	Pure or Distilled Water
1 tb.	Low-Sodium Tamari or Soy Sauce
2 tb.	Fresh chopped Basil, Tarragon or Parsley
1/2 ts.	Sea Salt, optional
dash	Cayenne Pepper
2 tb.	Arrowroot

Directions

1. In a sauce pot heat the oil and saute the onions and garlic to brown lightly.
2. Add the mushrooms, wine and sundried tomatoes and cook covered about 10 minutes.
3. Add the water and spices to the vegetables and simmer about 15 minutes, stirring occasionally.
4. Remove mushrooms with a slotted spoon. Combine arrowroot with 1/4 cup cool water, whip into sauce and simmer until sauce has thickened. Return mushrooms to the sauce.
5. Adjust spices as desired and serve.

Yield is approximately 3 cups

Breads
&
Snacks

Whole Wheat Raisin Bagels

For an easy breakfast, prepare and roll out the dough the night before, cover and refrigerate. In the morning, boil, bake and serve fresh from the oven.

3/4 cup	Pure or Distilled Water
3 tb.	Organic Apple Juice
2 ts.	Dry Yeast
1/2 ts.	Sea Salt
1 1/4 cups	Whole Wheat Pastry Flour
1 cup	Stoneground Whole Wheat Flour
1 ts.	Ground Cinnamon
2/3 cup	Organic Raisins
2 tb.	Barley Malt Syrup or Molasses

Directions

1. Combine together the first 4 ingredients in a large bowl or mixer.
2. Combine the flours, cinnamon and raisins with the liquid until smooth by using a dough hook, paddle or spoon.
3. Place mixture in an oiled bowl, cover with damp towel and let rest 1 hour.
4. In a large pot bring 2 1/2 quarts of water and the barley malt syrup to a boil.
5. While the water comes to boil, cut the rested dough into 6 equal pieces.
6. Roll the dough with the palms of your hands until it is uniform in diameter and about 10 inches in length. Shape the rolled dough into a circle, overlap the ends about 1 inch and form together.
7. Preheat oven to 400 degrees.
8. Add 3 bagels to the boiling water, when they rise to the top remove and place on a nonstick or lightly oiled sheet pan.
9. Repeat with the remaining bagels and bake 18-20 minutes until golden brown.
10. Allow to cool slightly before cutting with a serrated knife.

Yields 6 Bagels

Tex Mex Corn Bread

For a cookout or picnic try this spiced-up version of the classic cornbread.

1 1/2 cups	Rice Dream
1/4 cup	Fruit Source, sweetener and fat replacer
1/4 cup	Egg Replacer
1/4 cup	Canola Oil
1 tb.	Baking Powder
1 ts.	Sea Salt
1 cup	Yellow or White Cornmeal
1 cup	Whole Grain Pastry Flour
1 cup	Frozen Corn Kernels, thawed and drained
1 each	Red Pepper, diced 1/4 inch
1 each	Jalapeno Pepper, finely chopped without the seeds

Directions

1. Preheat oven to 375 degrees.
2. Combine the first 6 ingredients with a whip or mixer.
3. Add the cornmeal and flour until a smooth paste is formed.
4. Fold in the corn and peppers, pour into an oiled 8x10 pan and bake for 35-40 minutes, or until an inserted toothpick comes out clean.

Serves 6 - 8

If you like a thinner bread use a larger pan or for muffins pour into individual muffin tins.

Cilantro Aioli Croutons

You can decide which of your favorite whole grain breads
you would like to enhance.

1 each	Multi Grain Baguettte, sliced 1/2 inch thick or Whole Wheat Pita
1 bunch	Cilantro, rinsed, destemmed and chopped coarsely
1 ts.	Fresh minced Garlic
1 tb.	Lemon Juice
1/4 ts.	Sea Salt
dash	Cayenne Pepper
1/4 cup	Organic Cold Pressed Olive Oil

Directions

1. Preheat oven to 400 degrees.
2. Slice the bread or if using pita, split and cut into wedges.
3. Lay croutons or pita on a sheet pan and bake until golden, set aside to cool.
4. In a blender add the remaining 6 items and puree thoroughly.
5. Remove sauce from blender and brush over the croutons and serve.

This sauce will tend to discolor in the open air.
Please keep covered until needed.

Parmesan Crusted Croutons

*The finishing touch to French Onion Soup. You may want to make
a few extra. Somehow these delicious croutons seem
to disappear before the soup is ready! I wonder why?*

4 each	Sliced Whole Wheat Bread
3 oz.	Fat-Free Soy Mozzarella Cheese, shredded
4 tb.	Grated Soy Parmesan Cheese

Directions

1. Preheat oven to 400 degrees.
2. Place the bread on a sheet pan and bake about 10 minutes until lightly browned.
3. Remove the bread and flip over, return to oven and bake another 5 minutes until crispy.
4. Remove bread and cut in half diagonally, or trim to fit the size of the soup bowl.
5. Sprinkle the bread generously with the soy mozzarella cheese, then sprinkle on the soy parmesan cheese and place on a sheet pan.
6. Turn oven to the broil setting and 500 degrees.
7. Place the bread on the top rack and gratinee about 1/2 minute or until the cheese is lightly browned.

Serve warm on the top of French Onion Soup or as a snack.

Focaccia

Focaccia is a flat and flavorful Italian bread. It is wonderful with a salad or dinner.

Ingredients to make the dough:

3/4 cup	Pure or Distilled Water
2 ts.	Powdered Yeast
1/2 ts.	Sea Salt
3/4 cup	Whole Wheat Flour
3/4 cup	Whole Wheat Pastry Flour
1 ts.	Thyme or Rosemary Leaves

For the topping:

1 tb.	Cold Pressed Virgin Olive Oil
1 each	Medium Vidalia or Yellow Onion, peeled, halved and sliced 1/4 inch
1 ts.	Fresh minced Garlic
1 tb.	Rosemary Leaves
1/3 cup	Chopped Sundried Tomatoes, optional

Heat the oil to saute, add the vegetables and herbs, cook until tender and set aside.

Directions

1. Combine together the water, yeast and salt in a large bowl or mixer.
2. Combine the flours with the liquid until smooth, then fold in the thyme or rosemary.
3. Turn mix onto a floured table and knead for 2-3 minutes.
4. Place in an oiled bowl, cover and let rise 1 hour until the volume is almost doubled.
5. Preheat oven to 375 degrees while the bread rests. Saute the vegetables at this time.
6. Place dough onto a lightly floured table, cut in half and set one half aside.
7. With a rolling pin, roll out the dough into an 8-10 circle. It does not have to be perfect.
8. Place on a nonstick or slightly oiled baking sheet, sprinkle over half of the topping, let rise for a half hour, then bake 18-20 minutes until the crust is lightly browned.
9. Repeat with the remaining dough and topping and bake or freeze for a later date.

Yields 2 - 10 inch rounds

Parmesan Crusted Polenta

Polenta is made from water, cornmeal and spices and cooked on the stove top. When it cools, it can be cut into different shapes and can be grilled or broiled.

3 cups	Pure or Distilled Water or Low Fat Soy Milk
1 1/3 cups	Yellow or White Cornmeal
2 ts.	Fresh Minced Garlic
1/2 ts.	Sea Salt
1/8 ts.	Cayenne Pepper
1 ts.	Olive Oil or Canola Oil
1/2 cup	Soy Parmesan Cheese, "Lite n Less" by Soyco
2 cups	Marinara Sauce, optional

Directions

1. In a large sauce pan bring water to a boil.
2. Lower heat to medium and add the cornmeal slowly stirring with a wooden spoon.
3. Continue to stir the cornmeal adding the spices and simmer about 10 minutes until the mixture is very thick and difficult to stir. Be careful not to scorch the pot.
4. Lightly coat a 8 x 10 casserole dish with the olive oil and pour in the cornmeal mix.
5. Sprinkle the cheese over the cornmeal and bake at 425 degrees on the top rack of the oven, about 15-18 minutes or until the pie is golden on the top.
6. Remove and let cool slightly before cutting. Serve with your favorite marinara sauce.

Serves 4 - 6

For a Southwestern variation, add cut corn and diced red peppers to the cornmeal mix, sprinkle with fat-free soy monterey jack cheese with jalapenos and bake the same way.

Pita Croutons

The crunchiness of these croutons are habit-forming.
There are worse habits to have.

2 pieces	Whole Wheat Pita Bread
1 ts.	Minced Garlic
1 ts.	Dried Oregano Leaves
2 tb.	Organic Cold Pressed Olive Oil

Directions

1. Preheat oven to 400 degrees
2. Cut pita bread into 3/4 inch cubes and set aside.
3. Puree or whisk together olive oil, garlic and oregano.
4. Toss the oil mix a little at a time with the pita cubes. Spread the pita cubes evenly on a sheet pan.
5. Bake for 15-18 minutes or until brown and crispy. Cool and serve with soy parmesan cheese over your favorite soup or salad. It is also very good as a snack!

Yield is 1 1/2 cups

Whole Wheat Bread
with Basil and Sundried Tomatoes

This hearty bread is a healthy accompaniment to a salad or any meal for that matter.

1 1/2 cups	Distilled or Pure Water, luke-warm
1 tb.	Barley Malt Syrup
1 pkg.	Powdered Yeast
1 qt.	Whole Wheat Flour
1 tb.	Garlic Powder
1 bunch	Fresh chopped Basil
1/2 cup	Sundried Tomatoes, soak to soften and chop coarse

Directions

1. Combine together the water, yeast and barley malt syrup in a bowl and place on a warm stove.
2. Allow yeast to rise for 5 minutes.
   If the yeast does not react, try the procedure again with a fresh package of yeast.
3. In a mixer with a dough hook or in a large bowl combine the flours with the liquid until smooth, then fold in the herbs and tomatoes.
4. Turn mix onto a floured table and knead for 2-3 minutes.
5. Place in an oiled bowl, cover and let rise 1 hour until the volume is almost doubled.
6. Punch down, cover and let rise again, for about 1 hour.
7. Preheat oven to 375 degrees while the bread is rising.
8. Place half of the dough onto a lightly oiled loaf pan and bake approximately 45-50 minutes or until a nice firm crust has formed. You may also form the bread into baguette-style loaves by rolling out into a 10 inch long by 2 inch wide loaf and bake for about 25-30 minutes or until a firm crust develops on the bottom.
9. Allow to cool before cutting with a serrated knife.

Yields approximately 2 loaves or 4 baguettes

Vegetarian Roullade Sandwich

This colorful and nutritious sandwich is as much fun to make as it is to eat.

2 each	Soft Bread Sheets, available in natural food stores
1 qt.	Hummus with Roasted Red Peppers, recipe on page 15
1 bag	Fresh Spinach, cleaned and destemmed or Romaine Leaves
3 each	Vine Ripe Tomatoes, sliced in 1/4 inch slices
1 pint	Button Mushrooms, sliced 1/8 inch thin
2 cups	Shredded Carrots
1 pint	Alfalfa Sprouts

Directions

1. Prepare the hummus and process the vegetables. Place items in separate containers for an organized easy assembly.
2. Lay flat a soft flatbread directly in front of you on the work table. The wide part of the bread should be parallel to your abdomen.
3. Place all ingredients in order of the recipe on the other side of the flatbread.
4. Spread about 1 cup of hummus on the flatbread, leaving about 1 inch on the far side of the bread without the hummus to allow for overflow.
5. Arrange the spinach leaves over the hummus.
6. Now place a layer of each of the remaining items across the middle one third of the flatbread.
7. To roll, grasp with both hands the flat bread nearest and begin to roll. You may need to tuck the vegetables in the roll as you proceed.
8. When roll is complete, trim off the excess vegetables if there are any, for a clean look.
9. Slice the roll into one inch thick slices and serve with stoneground mustard, or creamy garlic dressing.

2 rolls can serve 4 - 6 guests

Desserts

Phyllo Pastry Desserts

This flaky pastry can replace pie dough and puff pastry and will surely be the talk of your dinner party. Upper left features Key Lime Mousse Tarts garnished with tofu whipped cream. The front plate is a delicious Raspberry Mango Strudel.

Apple Pear Phyllo Tarts

Your guests will always remember what they ate last at a dinner party.
They will not forget this crispy, low-fat tart.

2 each	D'Anjou Pears, peeled, cored and sliced in 1/2 inch slices
2 each	Granny Smith Apples, peeled, cored and sliced in 1/2 inch slices
2 tb.	Fresh Lemon Juice
2 ts.	Ground Cinnamon
1/2 ts.	Ground Nutmeg
1/3 cup	Organic Raisins
1/2 cup	Toasted Almond slices or slivers
1 box	Phyllo Dough, "Athens" is a recognizable name
1/3 cup	Canola Oil

Directions

1. Preheat oven to 375 degrees.
2. Combine the first 6 ingredients in a large mixing bowl.
3. Place mixture in a sauce pan, cover and simmer for 10 minutes until fruit is just tender.
4. Set mix aside and fold in the toasted almonds.

Tart Assembly

5. Open the phyllo and lay out the first two sheets on a clean, dry table.
6. With a pastry brush lightly brush the phyllo with the canola oil.
7. Lay two more sheets of pastry over the other two and brush with oil again.
8. Repeat again with two more layers of pastry and brush with oil again.
9. Lightly rub the inside of a large muffin pan with a paper towel and canola oil.
10. Cut the phyllo in 4 even squares and form a cup inside large muffin tins. Overlap parts of the pastry outside the muffin tins. Repeat procedure again for additional tarts.
11. Spoon fruit mixture into the phyllo cups about 2/3 full, fold over the outside pastry to enclose the tart. It does not have to be perfect.
12. Sprinkle the top with ground cinnamon and bake for 18-20 minutes, or until the top of the pastry is brown and crispy.
13. Remove tarts from oven, let cool for a couple minutes and remove from the tin carefully with a rubber spatula and serve.

Makes 4-6 tarts

For an added touch, line an entre plate with Tofu Sabayon Sauce and place the tart in the center.

Apple Cheese Crisp

*This warm dessert can be enjoyed by itself
or over Vanilla Rice Dream Ice Cream.*

Apple Filling

6 each	Red Delicious or Granny Smith Apples, peeled, cored and sliced 1/2 inch
2 each	Lemons, squeeze for juice
3/4 cup	Organic Raisins
1 ts.	Ground Cinnamon
2 tb.	Whole Wheat Flour
1/3 cup	Organic Apple Juice

Toss the apples and all other ingredients together and place in a casserole dish.

For the topping toss together:

1/3 cup	Organic Oatmeal Flakes
1/4 cup	Wheat Germ
1/4 cup	Whole Wheat Flour
1/2 cup	Chopped Walnuts or Pecans
2 oz.	Shredded fat-free Soy Cheddar Cheese
1/3 cup	Soy Margarine, melted

Directions

1. Preheat oven to 375 degrees.
2. Place the topping evenly over the apple filling and bake on the top rack 25-30 minutes or until browned and crispy.
3. Serve hot as is or use as a topping for Rice Dream ice cream.

Serves 4 - 6

*For variety, try using
pears or mangoes in place of the apples, or any combination of the three.*

Carob Chip Cookies

These cookies are scrumptious. They can be flavored with coconut or chopped nuts.

1/4 cup	Canola Oil
3/4 cup	Brown Rice Syrup
3 tb.	Pure or Distilled Water
1 tb.	Egg Replacer
1 tb.	Vanilla Extract
1 cup	Whole Wheat Flour
1 cup	Wheat Germ
1/2 ts.	Powdered Ginger, optional
1 cup	Unsweetened Carob Chips
1/2 cup	Unsweetened unrefined Coconut Flakes, optional
1/2 cup	Chopped Walnuts, Pecans or Macadamia Nuts, optional

Directions

1. Whip together the first 3 ingredients and egg replacer until smooth.
2. Blend in the flour, ginger and wheat germ.
3. Fold in the carob chips and the nuts or coconut until well blended.
4. Preheat oven to 325 degrees. Spoon the cookies onto an oiled sheet pan 1 inch apart.
5. Bake for 15-18 minutes until golden brown.

Makes about 18 cookies

Low Fat Carob Cake

This cake is low in saturated fat, natural sugar and of course cholesterol-free.

1 1/2 cups	Whole Grain Pastry Flour
3 tb.	Carob Powder or 4 tb. of low fat cocoa powder
2 ts.	Baking Powder
1/2 ts.	Sea Salt
3/4 cup	Soy Milk
2/3 cup	Brown Rice Syrup or Maple Syrup
1/3 cup	Canola Oil
1 ts.	Vanilla Extract
1/2 cup	Chopped Walnuts, Pecans or Macadamia Nuts, Optional

Directions

1. Preheat oven to 350 degrees.
2. In a mixing bowl combine the first 4 ingredients.
3. In a separate bowl whip together the remaining ingredients.
4. Add the wet mix to the dry mix and blend together until smooth.
5. Oil an 8-inch cake pan with canola oil and pour in batter.
6. Bake for 35 - 40 minutes or until the center is firm to touch.
7. Cool at room temperature before cutting.
    (Serve with a tofu whipped cream garnish.)

Serves 8 - 10

Mori Nu — the maker of most Silken Tofus, have a line of easy-to-prepare pudding mixes. They are also excellent to use as a healthy icing alternative.

Banana Ice Cream Pie

Made from only frozen bananas, you will need a Champion Juicer with the ice cream attachment to make this delicious dessert.

We use this pie to celebrate birthdays and other special occasions.

Pie Crust (Makes 2)

1 1/4 cups	Whole Almonds, slices or slivers can be substituted if whole are unavailable
2/3 cup	Organic Raisins
1 tb.	Carob Powder
1 ts.	Vanilla Extract
2 tb.	Brown Rice Syrup

Directions

1. In a food processor puree almonds, then add the remaining ingredients.
2. Press the crust mix into a 9 inch pie plate and up the sides of the plate.

220

Banana Ice Cream Pie *(continued)*
There are 2 different ways to prepare the filling:

A Champion juicer will provide the superior dessert and will be ready to serve quickly.

8 each   Ripe Bananas, peeled

Champion Juicer Method

1. When bananas have become very ripe, peel then freeze them for 8 hours or more.
2. Convert the juicer to the ice cream dispenser parts and push the frozen fruit through the chamber.
3. After all the fruit has been processed, spread evenly into pie shell.
4. Return pie to the freezer for a minimum of 2 hours, cut and serve.

You may choose many options for other flavors and garnishing. Such as:
Garnish the top of the pie by spreading tofu whipped cream and freeze again, before cutting. Fold in ground cinnamon, chopped nuts, coconut flakes, or carob chips into the filling before filling the pie shell.

Food Processor or Blender Method
This method is the less creamier of the two.

8 each   Ripe Bananas, peeled and cut into chunks
1/2 cup   Organic Apple Juice

Directions

1. Place the bananas and juice in a food processor and process until well blended.
2. Pour into pie shell and freeze overnight.
3. Remove pie from freezer about 30 minutes before cutting.

Garnish the same way as the first method, cut and serve.

Serves 8 per pie

Dessert Fruit Sauces

A colorful pool of fruit sauce on the bottom of a dessert plate truly adds to the presentation. All you need is a blender and a squeeze bottle to do what chefs have done for years in the finest restaurants.

1 cup	Fresh Strawberries or Kiwi, peeled and quartered
1/3 cup	Brown Rice Syrup

Directions

1. Place ingredients in a blender and puree until well blended.
2. Pour sauce onto the center of an entree plate and tilt the plate from side to side to coat evenly. You may also elect to pour the sauce into a squeeze bottle and squirt around the border of your dessert plate to decorate. Place your dessert in the center of the plate.

Sauce will hold refrigerated for 1 week or more.

You may also try other ripe fruits such as: peeled mangoes, papaya, peaches or raspberries.

Key Lime Mousse Tart

In honor of St. Patrick's Day we created this dairy-free dessert, similar in flavor to Key Lime Pie. The original version is laden with egg yolks and condensed milk, while this one is obviously cholesterol-free, much lower in fat and free of refined sugars.

20 oz.	Silken Tofu, extra firm, low-fat variety
1/3 cup	Fresh squeezed lime juice, Key Limes are the best if available
1 ts.	Finely grated lime rind
1/2 cup	Brown Rice Syrup

Directions

1. Drain and wipe dry the tofu with paper towels.
2. Break the tofu into cubes, place in blender with all ingredients, and whip until fluffy. If a thicker mousse is desired, add more tofu.
3. If you desire more tartness, add lime juice. For a sweeter mousse add more syrup.

Tart Assembly

1 pkg.	Phyllo Pastry
1/3 cup	Canola Oil
1/4 cup	Unsweetened shredded Coconut, toasted in the oven

1. Preheat oven to 375 degrees.
2. Lightly brush the inside of a large muffin pan with canola oil.
3. Open the phyllo and lay out the first two sheets on a clean, dry table.
4. With a pastry brush lightly brush the phyllo with the canola oil.
5. Lay two more sheets of pastry over the other two and brush with oil again.
6. Repeat again with two more layers of pastry and brush with oil again.
7. Cut the Phyllo sheet in 4 even squares and press into the inside of the muffin cups.
    Tuck outer parts of the pastry around the muffin tins to form a border.
8. Bake phyllo for 15-18 minutes or until brown and crisp. At the same time spread the coconut on a sheet pan and bake until golden brown.
9. Remove phyllo from the oven and cool at room temperature.
10. Place pastry on a dessert plate and fill with the chilled mousse.

Garnish with a sprinkle of toasted coconut, a rossette of tofu whipped cream, and a half slice of lime.

Serves 6 - 8

Light Lemon Cake

This cake was created with lemon lovers in mind.

1 cup	Whole Wheat Pastry Flour
1 cup	Unbleached White Flour
1 ts.	Baking Powder
1 ts.	Sea Salt
3/4 cup	Brown Rice or Maple Syrup
2/3 cup	Soy Milk
1/3 cup	Canola Oil
1/4 cup	Fresh Lemon Juice
1 tb.	Lemon Zest, obtain the zest from the lemons before squeezing
2 ts.	Lemon Extract
1/2 ts.	Lemon Oil, if unavailable add an additional 1/2 ts. of lemon extract
1 ts.	Vanilla Extract
1 ts.	Raw Apple Cider Vinegar *(acts as a leavening agent)*

Directions

1. Preheat oven to 350 degrees.
2. In a mixing bowl combine the first 4 ingredients.
3. In a separate bowl whip together the remaining ingredients.
4. Add the wet mix to the dry mix and blend together until smooth.
5. Oil (2) 8-inch or (1) 12-inch cake pan with canola oil and pour in batter.
6. Bake for 45 - 50 minutes or until the center is firm to touch.
7. Cool at room temperature before cutting.

Serve with a tofu whipped cream garnish. The Mori Nu brand Lemon Pie Filling also serves as an excellent healthy icing.

Serves 12 - 16

Phyllo Almond Rolls

This delicious dessert can also serve as a light breakfast or brunch pastry.

1 cup	Whole Almonds, chopped or buy slices or slivers
1 cup	Organic Raisins
1/4 cup	Soy Cream Cheese, available in natural food stores
1 tb.	Honey Sucanat Crystals, available in natural food stores
1 ts.	Cinnamon
1 box	Phyllo Pastry
1/3 cup	Canola Oil

Directions

1. Preheat oven to 375 degrees.
2. In a mixing bowl blend the first 5 ingredients together and set aside.
3. Open the phyllo and lay out the first two sheets on a clean, dry table.
4. With a pastry brush, lightly brush the phyllo with the canola oil.
5. Lay two more sheets of pastry over the other two and brush with oil again.
6. Place one third of the nut mixture evenly across one side of the pastry and roll the pastry over, resembling a jelly roll. Tuck outer sides of pastry under the rolled part.
7. Place pastry roll on a sheet pan, brush lightly with oil, dust with remaining cinnamon and with the tip of a knife, cut a few air pockets in the top of the pastry. Brush lightly with cool water.
8. Bake 18 - 20 minutes or until golden brown, remove from the oven and let cool.
9. Slice with a sharp knife and serve warm.

**Makes approximately 3 rolls,
1 roll will serve 4 - 6**

Luscious Lemon Pie

With assistance of my friend, vegetarian Chef Ken Hubscher,
this recipe was created.

1 1/2 cups	Oat Flour
1/2 cup	Toasted Sesame Seeds
1/4 cup	Canola Oil
1/4 cup	Brown Rice Syrup
2 ts.	Vanilla Extract
1/4 ts.	Sea Salt

Directions

1. Preheat oven to 375 degrees. Toast the sesame seeds about 18 minutes or until brown.
2. Mix the oat flour and toasted sesame seeds in a large bowl.
3. In a separate bowl whip together the remaining ingredients.
4. Combine the wet mix with the dry, being careful not to overmix.
5. Press the dough evenly, about 1/8 inch onto the bottom and sides of the pie shell. There may be enough dough for two shells.
6. Bake about 20 minutes or until the crust is brown. Cool pie crust in the refrigerator.

While the pie crust is baking, begin the preparation of the pie filling.

Luscious Lemon Pie *(continued)*

Pie Filling

1 cup	Organic Apple Juice
2 tb.	Agar Crystals
3/4 cup	Brown Rice Syrup
1/2 cup	Fresh Lemon Juice
pinch	Sea Salt
1/4 cup	2nd Apple Juice
2 tb.	Arrowroot, combine with 2nd apple juice until dissolved
1 ts.	Vanilla Extract
1 ts.	Lemon Zest, obtain by zesting the lemons before squeezing them for juice
1 cup	Tofu Whipped Cream, optional, recipe on page 238
1/4 cup	Toasted Coconut Flakes, optional

Directions

1. Puree the apple juice and agar in a blender. Transfer mixture to a pot and let rest for 15 minutes, stirring occasionally to dissolve.
2. Turn stove to low heat and slowly heat the juice mixture about 30 minutes, stirring frequently until dissolved. Place the mixture in a blender and puree.
3. Return to the pot, add the Brown Rice Syrup, salt and lemon juice, lemon zest and vanilla.
4. Bring to a boil and whip in the arrowroot mix and simmer until clear and dissolved.
5. Pour mixture into the baked pie crust and refrigerate 3-4 hours until filling is set.
6. Remove pie and spread a 1/2 inch layer of Tofu Whipped Cream over the pie.
7. Dust with toasted coconut flakes and garnish each slice with a half lemon slice.

Yields 2 - 8 inch pies

Burgundy Poached Pears

Two elegant, yet easy-to-prepare presentations of this alcohol-free dessert.

Burgundy Poached Pears

We celebrated Valentine's Day with this ruby-colored dessert.

4 each	D'Anjou Pears, Peeled and cored
2 tb.	Fresh Lemon Juice
1 bottle	Alcohol-Free Burgundy Wine
4 each	Cinnamon Sticks
1/2 cup	Organic Raisins
1/3 cup	Brown Rice Syrup
1 box	Firm Silken Tofu, Low-Fat , 10 oz. size

Directions

1. Bring the wine to a boil in a deep sauce pot.
2. Peel the pears and toss with the the lemon juice to prevent discoloring.
3. Place the cinnamon sticks and pears in the wine, cover and cook about 20 minutes, until pears are tender. Be careful not to overcook.
4. Remove the pears with a slotted spoon and refrigerate. Reserve the cooking liquid and cinnamon sticks.
5. While the wine is still hot pour over the raisins and allow to plump while the pears are cooling.
6. Strain the plumped raisins. Stuff the raisins inside the bottom of the pears.
7. In a blender puree 1 cup of the cooking wine, brown rice syrup and silken tofu.
8. Line an entree plate with the blended sauce and place the chilled pear in the center of the plate.
9. To garnish, insert the cooked cinnamon stick in the top of the pear to serve as the stem. Raspberries, blackberries or peppermint leaves as garnish will further dramatize the presentation.

You may also try Granny Smith Apples in place of the pears!

Serves 4

3-Seed Banana Cookies

This is a flour-free cookie that will keep you coming back for more!

12 each	Ripe Bananas, peeled and mashed
1 cup	Unsweetened Coconut Flakes
1 cup	Raisins
1/2 cup	Sesame Seeds, hulled
1/4 cup	Flax Seeds
1/4 cup	Sunflower Seeds, hulled

Directions
This recipe can be baked in a hydrolator or in an oven.

1. Turn on hydrolator or preheat oven to 200 degrees.
2. In a large bowl mash the bananas thoroughly.
2. Add the remaining ingredients and mix thoroughly.
3. With a teaspoon, scoop and form the cookies and place on the hydrolator racks or on a lightly oiled cookie sheet.
4. If using the hydrolator, allow to bake for 2 days or until the cookies are crispy.
   If using an oven bake for 6-8 hours or until crispy and lightly browned. We usually place them in the oven before going to bed. It makes for a nice morning surprise!

Approximate yield is 36 cookies

*For added variety you may try adding
oatmeal, almond slivers or any variety of chopped nuts !*

Pumpkin Phyllo Tarts

*A delicious Holiday treat, for Halloween, Thanksgiving
or any festive occasion !*

1/2 cup	Fruit Source or Sucanat, found in natural food stores
1/4 ts.	Sea Salt
1/2 ts.	Ground Cinnamon
1/4 ts.	Ground Nutmeg
1/8 ts.	Ground Ginger
2 tb.	Egg Replacer
12 oz.	Organic Pumpkin Pie Filling or other
8 oz.	Soy Milk or Almond Milk
1 box	Phyllo Dough, "Athens" is a recognizable name
1/2 cup	Canola Oil

Directions

1. Preheat oven to 375 degrees.
2. Combine the first 6 ingredients in a large mixing bowl thoroughly.
3. Add pumpkin and Soy Milk and continue mixing, then set aside.
4. Pour the pumpkin mix into a casserole dish and bake for 35 - 40 minutes.
5. Remove from oven, allow to cool in the refrigerator.

Tart Assembly

6. Open the phyllo and lay out the first two sheets on a clean, dry table.
7. With a pastry brush lightly brush the phyllo with the canola oil.
8. Lay two more sheets of pastry over the other two and brush with oil again.
9. Repeat again with two more layers of pastry and brush with oil again.
10. Lightly brush the inside of a large muffin pan with canola oil.
11. Cut the Phyllo in 4 even squares and form a cup inside the muffin tins.
  Tuck outer parts of the pastry around the muffin tins to form a border.
12. Bake phyllo for 15-18 minutes or until brown and crispy.
13. Remove phyllo from oven and cool at room temperature.
14. Place pastry on a tray and fill with cooled pumpkin mix about 1 inch .

Garnish with tofu whipped cream and dust the top of the tart with cinnamon.
Serves 6 - 8

Almost Rum Balls

You will find this holiday dessert can be a wonderful
"petit four" throughout the year.

1 1/4 cups	Whole Almonds, slices or slivers can be substituted if whole almonds are unavailable
2/3 cup	Organic Raisins or Medjoul Dates that have the seeds removed
1 tb.	Carob Powder
1 tb.	Vanilla Extract
2 tb.	Brown Rice Syrup

Directions

1. In a food processor puree the almonds, then add the remaining ingredients until well blended.
2. Form the mixture into little balls, 1 inch in diameter and roll with the palms of your hand.
   If you use your fingers too much, the balls will not be uniformly round.
3. Coat the balls with carob powder, coconut flakes or crushed nuts and serve.

Yield is approximately 2 dozen

Frozen Strawberry Pie

*This low-cal dessert must be prepared a day in advance
in order to freeze completely.*

Pie Crust

1 1/4 cups	Whole Almonds, slices or slivers can be substituted if whole are unavailable
2/3 cup	Organic Raisins
1 tb.	Carob Powder
1 ts.	Vanilla Extract
2 tb.	Brown Rice Syrup

Directions

1. In a food processor puree almonds, then add the remaining ingredients.
2. Press the crust mix into a 9-inch pie plate and up the sides of the plate.

Pie Filling

3 pints	Strawberries, destemmed, rinsed and sliced 1/4 inch thick or try Kiwi, peeled and sliced, layer it the same as you would strawberries
1 cup	Diced Pineapple, peeled, cored and cut into 2 inch cubes
2/3 cup	Organic Apple Juice
1 ts.	Ground Cinnamon

Directions

1. Slice strawberries and set aside for future assembly.
2. Place apple juice in a blender, add the pineapple and cinnamon and puree.

Assembly Instructions

1. Place a full layer of sliced strawberries over the pie crust.
2. Pour enough of the fruit puree over the strawberries to coat.
3. Add another layer of strawberries.
4. Pour another layer of fruit puree evenly over the strawberries.
5. Place the final layer of strawberries over the fruit puree.
6. Spread the remaining fruit puree over the berries, cover with plastic and freeze overnight.
7. To serve, remove the pie from the freezer 30-45 minutes before cutting.
8. Carefully cut the frozen pie and serve with a pie spatula.

Serves 8

Papaya Blackberry Phyllo Strudel

If blackberries are unavailable, try using fresh blueberries.

1 box	Phyllo Pastry
2 tb.	Canola Oil
2 each	Ripe Papayas, peeled, seeded and cut into 1/2 inch cubes
1 pint	Blackberries
2 tb.	Brown Rice Syrup (only if the raspberries are too sour for you)
2 ts.	Ground Cinnamon

A word of caution: Phyllo is a very delicate, low-fat pastry. Its worst enemies are air and water. Be sure your work surface is dry, and while working with the pastry cover the unused portion with a towel or plastic wrap. When exposed to air, the pastry will dry out quickly and break very easily.

Directions

1. Preheat oven to 375 degrees.
2. Lightly toss the papayas, berries, syrup and cinnamon in a bowl and set aside.
3. Open the phyllo and lay out the first two sheets on a clean, dry table.
4. With a pastry brush lightly brush the phyllo with the canola oil.
5. Lay two more sheets of pastry over the other two and brush with oil again.
6. Repeat again with two more layers of pastry and brush with oil.
7. Spoon the fruit mixture evenly along one side of the pastry and roll the pastry over the fruit resembling a jelly roll. Tuck outer sides of pastry under the rolled part.
8. Place on a sheet pan, brush lightly with oil, dust with remaining cinnamon and with the tip of a knife, cut a few air pockets in the top of the pastry. Brush lightly with cool water.
9. Bake 20-25 minutes or until golden brown, remove from oven and let cool.
10. Slice on an angle with a sharp knife and serve warm.

1 roll will serve 4 - 6

If there are leftovers, which doesn't happen very often, you may reheat in the oven the following day and the pastry will become crispy again.

Baked Pears in Phyllo

The height of this dessert truly adds to the presentation of this plate.

4 each	D'Anjou Pears, peeled and cored through the bottom
2 tb.	Fresh Lemon Juice
2 cups	Organic Apple Juice
4 each	Cinnamon Sticks
1/3 cup	Organic Raisins
1 ts.	Ground Cinnamon
1 box	Phyllo Pastry
2 tb.	Canola Oil

Directions

1. Bring the apple juice to a boil in a sauce pot while peeling the pears.
2. Lightly toss the pears in the lemon juice to prevent discoloring.
3. Place the cinnamon sticks and pears in the hot apple juice, cover and cook about 15 minutes or until slighly tender. Do not overcook.
4. Remove the pears with a slotted spoon and set aside to cool. Then stuff the bottom of the pears with the raisins.
5. Preheat oven to 375 degrees.
6. On a clean dry table, open the phyllo and lay out the first two sheets.
7. With a pastry brush lightly brush the phyllo with the canola oil.
8. Cut the sheet in half twice to make 4 squares. Place the brushed phyllo squares on top of each other.
9. Place the poached pear on the center of the phyllo square, dust with cinnamon and enclose the pear with the pastry.
10. Brush the outside of the pastry lightly with oil and place on a sheet pan, dust with remaining cinnamon and bake about 25 minutes, or until golden brown.
11. Remove from oven, cool slightly and serve warm.

For an elegant presentation, place about 2 ounces of Tofu Sabayon Sauce on a large entre plate and swirl around the plate to coat evenly. Place the pear in the center of the plate and surround with raspberries spaced about 2 inches apart around the plate.

Serves 4

If there are leftovers, you may reheat in a 375 degree oven for 10-12 minutes and the pastry will become crispy again. You may also try Granny Smith Apples in place of the pears!

Raspberry Mango Phyllo Strudel

This is an exciting but light alternative to the traditional puff pastry strudels.

1 box	Phyllo Pastry
2 tb.	Canola Oil
2 each	Ripe Mangoes, peeled, seeded and cut into 1/2 inch cubes
1 pint	Raspberries
2 tb.	Brown Rice Syrup (only if the raspberries are too sour for you)
2 ts.	Ground Cinnamon

Directions

1. Preheat oven to 375 degrees.
2. Lightly toss the mangoes, berries, syrup and cinnamon in a bowl and set aside.
3. Open the phyllo and lay out the first two sheets on a clean, dry table.
4. With a pastry brush lightly brush the phyllo with the canola oil.
5. Lay two more sheets of pastry over the other two and brush with oil again.
6. Repeat again with two more layers of pastry and brush with oil.
7. Place the fruit mixture evenly across one side of the pastry and roll the pastry over the fruit, resembling a jelly roll. Tuck outer sides of pastry under rolled part.
8. Place on a sheet pan, brush lightly with oil, dust with remaining cinnamon and, with the tip of a knife, cut a few air pockets in the top of the pastry. Brush lightly with cool water.
9. Bake 20-25 minutes or until golden brown, remove from oven and let cool.
10. Slice on an angle with a sharp knife and serve warm.

1 roll will serve 4 - 6

Tofy Sabayon Sauce, recipe on page 239, will provide a nice vanilla sauce accompaniment to the strudel.

Really Rice Pudding

Not only is brown rice the main ingredient, we have used rice milk and brown rice syrup as the next 2 ingredients of importance.

1 qt.	Pure or Distilled Water
2 cups	Short Grain Brown Rice, place in a strainer and rinse with cool water
2 2/3 cups	Rice Dream or Almond Milk
3/4 cup	Brown Rice Syrup
3/4 cup	Organic Raisins
1 tb.	Fresh Lemon Zest
1 tb.	Vanilla Extract
1 ts.	Ground Cinnamon
1/2 ts.	Ground Nutmeg

Directions

1. In a large pot bring the water to a boil, add the brown rice, cover and cook 30-35 minutes or until the liquid has evaporated.
2. Fold in the remaining ingredients, lower heat to simmer and cook uncovered until most of the liquid has evaporated.
3. Pour mixture into a casserole dish and refrigerate until chilled.
4. Garnish with ground cinnamon and serve.

Serves 6 - 8

Tofu Whipped Cream

You will be pleasantly surprised with the flavor and fluffiness of this healthier version of whipped cream.

8 oz.	Extra Firm Silken Tofu, low fat variety
1 tb.	Canola Oil
2 tb.	Honey, Brown Rice Syrup, or Maple Syrup
2 ts.	Fresh Lemon Juice
1 ts.	Vanilla Extract

Directions

1. Drain and blot dry the tofu with paper towels.
2. Break the tofu into cubes, place in a blender with all ingredients, and whip until fluffy. Turn the blender off and scrape down the sides to be sure no tofu chunks are remaining and puree until smooth.

Yield 1 1/2 cups

For a thicker cream, add more tofu, for a thinner one, add more lemon juice. Many thanks to Gloria Wilburn for providing this recipe.

Chocolate Tofu Mousse

1 1/2 cups	Tofu Whipped Cream
1 1/2 tb.	Low Fat Cocoa Powder or Carob Powder or
1 cup	Strawberries, destemmed and halved to make Strawberry Mousse
1 cup	Kiwi, peeled and cubed for Kiwi Mousse

Place ingredients in blender and puree. Serve well chilled.

Tofu Sabayon Sauce

This low-fat, cholesterol-free version of the French vanilla dessert sauce or, as the Italians call it, Zabaglione is also easier to prepare. Just thinking about the days of using heavy cream and egg yolks to prepare this sauce makes me cringe! This recipe sure gives me a lot of peace of mind when serving.

8 oz.	Firm or Extra Firm Silken Tofu, low-fat variety
1/2 cup	Vanilla Soy Milk, Almond Mylk or Rice Dream
pinch	Saffron Threads
1/3 cup	Brown Rice Syrup
1 ts.	Vanilla Extract

Directions

1. Drain and blot dry the tofu with paper towels and break into cubes.
2. Place tofu in a blender with all ingredients and puree until smooth.

Adjust the consistency of the sauce with tofu to thicken or with soy milk to thin out.

Yield about 1 1/2 cups

This sauce serves as tasty and colorful sauce base below a fruit phyllo strudel or tart !

Very Vanilla Cake

This easy to prepare cake can be made lighter by using water or rice milk in place of the soy milk.

1 3/4 cup	Whole Wheat Pastry Flour
1 ts.	Baking Powder
1 ts.	Baking Soda
1/2 ts.	Sea Salt
3/4 cup	Brown Rice or Maple Syrup
2/3 cup	Soy Milk, Rice Milk or Water
1/3 cup	Canola Oil
2 tb.	Vanilla Extract
1 tb.	Raw Apple Cider Vinegar *(acts as a leavening agent)*

Directions

1. Preheat oven to 350 degrees.
2. In a mixing bowl combine the first 4 ingredients.
3. In a separate bowl whip together the remaining ingredients.
4. Add the wet mix to the dry mix and blend together until smooth.
5. Oil an 8-inch cake pan with canola oil and pour in batter.
6. Bake 35 - 40 minutes or until the center is firm to touch.
7. Cool at room temperature before cutting.

Serve with a tofu whipped cream garnish. The Mori Nu brand Lemon Pie Filling makes an nice healthy icing.

Serves 8 - 10

Sample Menus

To assist with a well-rounded meal program,
we have listed a typical lunch menu and 4 weeks of dinner menus.
There is also a Kid's Vegetarian Favorites (asterisk *) placed beside
those items in the index in the back of the book.

LUNCH MENU

Reference Pages

Day		Reference Pages
Sunday	Scrambled Tofu with Curry, Peppers and Scallions	100
	Fresh Baked Bread with Sundried Tomato Tapenade or	200
	Baked Home Fried Potatoes	128
Monday	Tossed Salad with Low-Fat Dressings, Baked Potatoes with Soy Cheddar Cheese and Avocados	
Tuesday	Create Your Pita Sandwich with Black Bean Hummus Assorted Sprouts and Vegetables	6
Wednesday	Garden Salad with Creamy Garlic Dressing	60
	Greek Pasta Salad	16
Thursday	Waldorf Salad on a bed of Romaine Lettuce	28
	Banana Ice Cream Pie	20
Friday	Green Leaf Salad with Assorted Sprouts and Nuts Mustard Tahini Dressing	68
Saturday	Caesar Salad with Pita Croutons and Baked Potato with Stoneground Mustard or Baked Sweet Potato	8

DINNER MENU
Week 1

		Reference Pages
Sunday	Vegetable Sushi Roll with Seaweed Cole Slaw and	117, 20
	Stir Fried Tofu and Vegetables	104
Monday	Black & White Bean Soup with Cilantro Aioli Croutons	34, 48, 208
	Garden Salad with Avocado Cucumber Dressing	56
	Pasta with Wild Mushroom Ragout	88
Tuesday	Caesar Salad with Pita Croutons	8
	Baked Potato Skins with Fat-Free Soy Cheddar Cheese	132
	Soy Sour Cream and Fresh Vegetable Medley	
Wednesday	Field Greens with Raspberry Tahini Dressing	75
	Brown Rice and Lentil Stew with Grilled Vegetables	114
Thursday	Jicama Orange Salad with Peppermint	18
	Vegetable Quesadillas with Mexican Salsa and	148, 195
	Guacamole	61
Friday	Spinach Salad with Pineapple Mustard Dressing	70
	Vegetable Lasagne Marinara with Green Beans Lyonnaise	86, 169
Saturday	Spring Vegetable Soup	52
	Tossed Salad with Lemon Mustard Dressing	64
	Vegetable Pita Pizza	144

DINNER MENU

		Reference Pages
Sunday	Vine-Ripe Tomatoes and Soy Mozzarella with Pesto Sauce	25
	Shepherd's Pie, Steamed Sugar Snap Peas and Tangy Carrots	130, 164
Monday	Fat-Free Cucumber Dill Salad	13
	Vegetable Chili with Cilantro over Steamed Brown Rice	138
Tuesday	Louisiana Corn Chowder	38
	Tossed Salad with Fat-Free Italian Dressing	62
	Cajun Grilled Tofu Steaks and Okra with Stewed Tomatoes	103, 182
Wednesday	Garden Salad with Creamy Italian Dressing	63
	Pasta with Sundried Tomatoes, Wild Mushrooms and Pesto Sauce	84
Thursday	Portabella Mushroom Burger on a 6-Grain Roll	145
	with Alfalfa Sprouts, Lettuce and Tomato and Oven Fried Sweet Potatoes	128
Friday	Mesclun Lettuce Salad with Creamy French Dressing	60
	Grilled Vegetable Burritos with Mexican Salsa	134, 195
	Red Beans and Rice	115
Saturday	Heart to Heart Salad	17
	Eggplant Parmesan with Marinara Sauce	108
	and Italian Spinach Saute	173

DINNER MENU

Week 3

DINNER MENU
Week 4

Reference
Pages

Day	Menu	Pages
Sunday	Minestrone Soup	45
	Angel Hair Pasta Pomodori Salad	2
Monday	Garden Salad with Miso Dressing	67
	Vegetable Spring Roll with Mango Duck Sauce	154, 193
	Broccoli with Garlic, Tamari and Coconut Sauce	159
Tuesday	Spinach Salad with Citrus Poppyseed Dressing	58
	Red Bean and Tofu Enchiladas with Mexican Salsa	106, 195
	and Grilled Vegetable Salad	26
Wednesday	"Fire & Ice Salad" (Marinated Tomatoes and Cucumbers)	14
	Herbed New Potatoes, Corn on the Cob	127
	and Zucchini withs Fines Herbes	181
Thursday	Caesar Salad with Pita Croutons	8
	Whole Wheat Angel Hair Pasta with Tofu Meatballs	102
	and Marinara Sauce	194
Friday	Meatless Chili Taco Salad with Baked Tortilla Chips	40
	Grated Fat-Free Soy Cheddar Cheese, Diced Onions	
	Shredded Romaine Lettuce and Mexican Vinaigrette	66
Saturday	Field Greens Salad with Sundried Tomato Vinaigrette	73
	Penne Pasta Primavera with Tofu Alfredo Sauce	89, 184

245

Acknowledgements

Kelp, Dulse and other Sea Supplements,
by William H. Lee, Keats Publishing, 1983

Grain Power
by Beatrice Trum Hunter, Keats Publishing, 1994

Tofu, Tempeh, Miso and other Soyfoods
by Richard Levitron, Keats Publishing, 1982

Miami Herald
Pam Smith O'Hara, May 1995

Vegetarian Times, Vegan Pasta
by Bryanna Clark Grogan, June 1995

Tofu Cookery
by Louise Hagler, The Book Publishing, 1991

Fasting with Juices
by Steve Meyerowitz, The Sprout House, 1992

Simplifying Sushi
by Dana Jacobi, Natural Health, March 1996

Friendly Foods
by Brother Ron Pickarski, Ten Speed Press, 1991

Glossary

Agar   An Oriental seaweed that can be used as a vegan substitute for gelatin, which is an animal product. Agar is used mainly as a thickener when making fruit jellies, pies and aspic molds. It is rich in calcium, iron, vitamins A, B-complex, C, D and iodine. Because it adds bulk to any meal without calories, agar is helpful in curbing appetite when dieting.

Aioli   A garlic mayonnaise that has its roots in Provence, France. It can be used to garnish bean soups, to enhance grilled or steamed vegetables or as a flavorful butter substitute with fresh breads.

Al dente   Italian for literally "to the bite". Al dente is commonly used to describe the texture of pasta or vegetables that are cooked until firm or crunchy, not soft and overdone.

Angel Hair   The thinnest pasta, too fine to be cut by hand. A popular pasta for the health conscious.

Arame   A mildly flavored sea vegetable that is very easy to use. It is shaped in short dark strands and can be softened in warm water and ready to use in minutes. Because it is delicate, be careful not to oversoak or overhandle it as arame will fall apart very easily.

Arrowroot   A powdered flour from the root of a tropical plant. It can be used in cooking to replace cornstarch which is chemically processed. Arrowroot remains clear when added to thicken a sauce, and is easily digested. Be sure to dissolve it first in water.

Baguette   A long cylindrical loaf of French bread.

Balsamic Vinegar   An Italian vinegar made from fermented grapes. Not as sour as traditional vinegars, balsamic actually tends to be almost sweet. The longer the balsamic is aged, sometimes as long as 80 years, the richer and sweeter the flavor will be. The town of Modena, Italy is the birthplace of this vinegar.

Barley Malt Syrup   A natural sweetener made from sprouted whole barley. It has a caramel flavor and color. Compared to molasses , honey or maple syrups, barley malt syrup has 75% less natural sugar content.

Basil   A pungent herb from the mint family used extensively in Mediterranean cooking.

Blackstrap   A dark heavy molasses, low in flavor, but very nutritious.

Bok Choy   A Chinese white cabbage with thick white stems and chard-like leaves. Often used in stir-fry dishes and Oriental salads.

Bouquet Garni A bunch of herbs tied together, usually in cheesecloth and added to soups or sauces as they cook. It usually includes bay leaf, thyme, peppercorns, parsley and whatever herbs you may desire.

Bragg Liquid Aminos A vegetarian low-sodium replacement for low-sodium soy sauce or tamari. Bragg has about 25% less sodium than low-sodium soy sauce products.

Brown Rice Syrup A light and delicate natural sweetener made from brown rice and water. Use to sweeten dressings and dessert sauces, brown rice syrup has about 75% less natural sugar content than honey or maple syrups. Over 50% of brown rice syrup is made of complex sugars, which means our body has to break it down to a simple sugar before it penetrates our bloodstream. This helps to curve those sugar highs and lows that are common with refined sugar products.

Buckwheat Flour A native of the sorrel and rhubarb family, not a true cereal grain. It is used to make Japanese soba noodles and Russian pancakes known as blinis.

Bulgur Cracked wheat that has been hulled, parboiled and dried. This nutty textured cereal is popular in taboulleh, pilaf and kasha varnishkes. To cook, simply pour boiling water over the bulgur, cover and let stand for about 15 minutes or until tender.

Caper Everyone always wants to ask "What is a caper?" Native to Africa and the Mediterranean, the caper is a bud or young fruit of a climbing plant. It is then pickled in a tart brine and served as a condiment in seafood, pasta and is also used in the classic Piccata sauce, which is made with lemon, white wine and butter. Nonparielles are the small pickled capers from Provence, France. They are the finest quality capers.

Carob From an evergreen tree whose pods are eaten both fresh and dried. It is high in protein and sugar and can be found in powder form or chips. There are unsweetened carob chips now available in natural food stores.

Casaba A large winter melon or muskmelon with ribbed skin, pale flesh which when ripened, has a very sweet flavor and soft flesh.

Cayenne Pepper Red chili pepper, dried and ground powdery fine. A native of Mexico, cayenne is very hot, rich in vitamins A and C and is a natural body cleanser.

Chili The fruit of the pepper plant, native of the Capsicum family. Its heat index ranges from mild to fiery hot.

Chive An herb of the onion family, its tall thin green stems are sliced and used to add color and a delicate onion flavor to soups, salads and sauces.

Cilantro   An essential herb in cuisines from around the world. From Bangkok to the Yucatan , this pale green herb looks like parsley, but its leaves are feathery and flat. Cilantro has a sharp, almost lemony flavor and a peppery aroma. In the U.S. its nickname is "Mexican parsley". Cilantro is the dominant spice in Mexican salsa.

Coriander   An herb valued for its dried seeds. Used extensively in Oriental, Indian and Spanish cooking, the Spanish word for coriander is cilantro. The flavor of coriander resembles a combination of sage, caraway and lemon.

Cornstarch   A chemically processed white flour milled from corn, used extensively as a thickening agent in Chinese cooking. Arrowroot is a much healthier alternative for thickening sauces.

Coulis   An old culinary term that has undergone a few definition changes. It now means a thick sauce or puree of fruits or vegetables such as tomatoes or raspberries.

Couscous   A Moroccan dish consisting of semolina flour, a refined durum wheat. Healthier types of couscous such as durum semolina couscous or whole wheat couscous in are now available in natural food stores. They are high in fiber and are more nutritious products. Couscous is typically steamed on the top of a two part pot that has vegetables or meats cooking below.

Cumin   A spice made from the seeds of the cumin plant and a relative of the parsley family. Cumin is used generously in most European, Middle Eastern and Asian countries.

Curry   A mixture of spices used in Indian cooking for thousands of years. It consists of a vast array of savory spices ranging from cardamom, cinnamon, chilis, cloves, coriander, cumin, fennel seed, garlic, mace, nutmeg, poppy and sesame seeds, tamarind and tumeric.

Daikon   A large radish, off-white in color and longer and larger than a carrot or parsnip. Daikon is used extensively in Japanese cooking either raw or cooked.

Dulse   A nutritious sea vegetable that is purple-red in color and fast cooking. It can be used in any recipe calling for wakame, but it is much more fragile to handle. Dulse has one of the highest natural sources of iron of any known food source. It is also very rich in potassium for kidney function and magnesium for RNA and DNA production.

Durum Wheat   The hardest species of wheat, usually made into semolina flour.

Egg Replacer   *A powdered egg substitute used for replacing eggs in baking recipes and even crepes. It is made primarily from potato starch and tapioca flour and is an animal-free product.*

Enchilada   *A tortilla that has been filled with vegetables, cheese or meats and baked or fried and served with Mexican-style sauces.*

Falafel   *Dried chick peas or fava beans that are spiced, shaped into balls or patties and deep-fried. Eaten throughout the Middle East with some variations.*

Fennel   *An an anise-flavored vegetable or herb used prevalently in Mediterranean cooking. Its bulbous stems, leaves and seeds are edible.*

Fructose   *The form of sugar found in many plants, especially fruit and honey. It tastes sweeter than sucrose and contains half as many calories. It is not necessarily more healthful or natural than other forms of sugar, especially when crystallized.*

Fruit Source   *A powdered form of white grapes and brown rice syrup crystals. It is used to sweeten and also act as a fat replacer in baking.*

Garbanzo Beans   *Also known as chick peas, they are a legume that is a good source of protein and carbohydrates. It can also be found in flour form or in miso.*

Gluten   *A substance formed when certain flours, especially hard wheat, are combined with water and yeast and made into an elastic dough. It then rises due to the trapped air bubbles produced by the yeast. Gluten can be found in flours usually reserved for bread making. Gluten flour is pure gluten and all protein with no carbohydrates.*

Grill   *To cook over flames, coals or embers, or under a broiler using intense direct heat.*

Guacamole   *Avocado mashed with onion, chilis, lemon juice, spices and tomatoes. Can be served as a dip, filling or sauce.*

Haricot Verte   *A thin green bean very popular in French cooking.*

Hijiki   *Is a strong-flavored sea vegetable, darker in color and quite dirty. Hijiki must be washed carefully. It can be delicious cooked with onions and tofu, or used to compliment greens, soups or salads.Most prefer the milder and less labor intensive arame or wakame.*

Hull   *To husk or remove the outer covering of a seed or fruit or the pith such as the green top of a strawberry.*

Hummus   Chick peas or other legumes mashed into a paste with lemon juice and garlic. It can be flavored with tahini and other spices such as cumin and pepper and is eaten traditionally with pita bread and vegetables.

Jalapeno   A green chili pepper, about 2 inches long, that can be very hot. It is used fresh or can be found pickled in jars.

Jerusalem Artichoke A root vegetable of the sunflower plant. It is not related to artichokes, nor is it from Jerusalem. This tuber is dark in color, small, white and sweet. They do not contain starch and can be found in more nutritious pastas, deep-fried or stir-fried dishes. The inulin found in this vegetable has many health benefits of which one is helping to keep our blood sugar in balance.

Jicama   A root vegetable that is crispy and slightly sweet. It has a tan flaky skin and the meat is white. Jicama can be used raw, shredded or julienned in salads or cooked as a vegetable side dish.

Kale   A loose, green leafy vegetable of the cabbage family. It is highly nutritious and is a very durable vegetable that holds up well when cooked or stewed.

Kamut   Kamut is an ancient grain thought to be an ancestor of modern hybrid wheat. Like spelt, kamut was introduced in the U.S. so recently that the grain has not been included in the USDA's analysis. However, recent studies show kamut contains 20-40 percent more protein than common varieties of wheat. When cooked, its crunchy kernels are wonderful served as a pilaf or sprinkled over a tossed salad.

Kasha   Roasted buckwheat that originated in the Soviet Union. It is flaky when cooked and heartier in flavor than groats.

Kelp   A sea vegetable that is a potent source of natural iodine. Available in powdered form, kelp can be used as a salt substitute In its dried form, kelp can be used in soups, stews, vegetables or baked or fried until crispy for a snack.

Kiwi   A small tree of Chinese origin , plum shaped, with a brown fuzz for skin and a bright green center with attractive black seeds. Its flavor resembles a sweet tart, a cross somewhere between a strawberry and honeydew melon. It has gained most of its notoriety and fame from the Australian marketing.

Kombu   Kombu is dried kelp. It can be found in strips or in flakes. Add kombu strips to soup stocks for flavor, or to bean soups to improve flavor and aid digestion. Once it is cooked and has expanded, remove kombu from the stock, let cool and slice into strips and return to the soup.

Kuzu   Kuzu is a concentrated starch from the kudzu plant. It can be found in powder or stones and is used as a thickener, similar to arrowroot and cornstarch. It is much more expensive than arrowroot. In Japan it is used for medicinal purposes. Macrobiotically, kuzu is referred to as a yang starch.

Legume   The seed pod of leguminous plants whose peas or beans are eaten fresh, sprouted or dried and possess a high protein and carbohydrate value. Any of the beans, split peas or lentils are from the legume family, and can be a a good source of dietary fiber.

Lemon Grass   Stems from a leafy green plant known as sorrel, which is similar to spinach, but has a lemony-flavor. Lemon grass actually is a variety called "wild sorrel", which is known for its high oxalic acid content.

Lyonnaise   French for sauces containing onions. The onions are usually sauteed in butter or oil, and reduced with white wine or vinegar.

Mace   A spice made from the lacy covering of the nutmeg seed. It is dried to an orange brown color and powdered. Mace tastes like nutmeg, with a hint of cinnamon.

Mango   The fruit of a tropical evergreen tree of Indian or Malayan origin. Deep orange in color, a fully-ripened mango is one of the most delicious fruits you will ever savor. It is also a rich source of beta-carotene.

Marjoram   A Mediterranean herb from the mint family, somewhat sweet in flavor.

Mesclun   A French Provencal mixture of young salad greens. It includes wild chicory, mache, curly escarole, dandelion and radicchio.

Mesquite   A scrub tree that grows wild in the southwestern U.S. and Mexico. Its wood has become very useful in adding smoked flavor to grilled food.

Mint   An aromatic Mediterranean herb that includes basil, marjoram, oregano, peppermint, rosemary, sage, savory and thyme in its large family. Common garden mint is spearmint. Did you know that mint has never been highly regarded by French chefs ?

Millet   A grain native to Africa and Asia. It is a gluten-free grain that is a high protein staple. In the U.S. it is mostly used for animal fodder, but it is gaining in popularity in the vegetarian diet.

Miso   One of the oldest condiments known to man. Miso is made from a fermented paste made from beans or grains and salt. It contains 10-12% protein. It is a pre-digested food that is a remarkable digestive aid. Miso can be used as a flavoring agent for soups, dressings, sauces, vegetables and soy foods and comes in a wide variety of flavors and colors. You really should experiment with the many flavors of miso that are available in natural food stores. When miso is added to a hot soup, try to consume it within 5-10 minutes to receive the maximum digestive benefits.

Molasses   The syrup remaining from sugar cane juice after sucrose crystallization. This process is repeated three times, each yielding a lower grade of molasses with more impurities and darker color from the high heat. Blackstrap is the third grade.

MSG   A controversial seasoning that is made of sodium and glutamic acid. It was chemically isolated from a sea vegetable in the early 1900's and is held in high esteem by commercial food manufacturers to inexpensively flavor everything from soups to nuts. MSG has been known to affect the central nervous system and cause discomfort to asthma and migraine sufferers.

One must exercise caution when reading labels. MSG is listed by a variety of different names such as: autolyzed yeast extract, hydrolyzed vegetable protein or HVP, potassium glutamate, sodium caseinate, broth, natural or artificial flavorings. Some tuna fish packaged in vegetable "broth" contains glutamic acid.

Nori   A high-protein red seaweed that is sometimes dyed. In the U.S. nori is used mostly as the paper thin wrapper in which sushi is rolled. In Asian countries it is used as a condiment or as a main dish. Avoid buying nori sheets that are a uniform green. Choose those that are multi-hued in color.

Organic   Refers to produce grown without artificial or chemical fertilizers or pesticides.

Oregano   Wild marjoram, an herb especially popular in Italian cooking. Oregano is very similar to marjoram but more pungent.

Okra   A tropical plant of the mallow family, native to Africa and Asia. Brought to the southern U.S. with the slave trade; okra is used as a vegetable and a thickener for soups because of its gelatinous texture when cooked.

Orzo   A rice-shaped pasta popular in Italy and Greece.

Papaya   A tall tropical plant native to America; its large pear shaped fruit has a thin skin that turns yellow when ripe. Unripened papaya can be cooked as a vegetable similar to squash. The most popular papaya is ripened . Its sweet, soft orange flesh is one of the most delectable fruits there are, and a rich source of beta-carotene. Its black seeds are inedible and resemble peppercorns; they can be removed with a teaspoon.

Parsley   An herb known to the ancient Greeks and Romans for its medicinal properties, but now used strictly for culinary purposes. Curly leaf parsley is popular in the U.S. and the more pungent flat leaf or Italian parsley is more popular in Europe.

Peanut   Not a true nut but the seed of a leguminous bush native to South America and highly nutritious.

Pearl Barley   Hulled and polished barley, small and round like pearls, and eaten in soups or pilafs as you would rice.

Penne   Quill-shaped pasta that is tubular and cut diagonally.

Pesto   A sauce from Genoa of crushed basil, garlic, pine nuts, parmesan and olive oil. It is a robust and addictive sauce used to enhance pasta, soups and vegetables.

Plantain   A fruit closely related to the banana, but whose higher starch and lower sugar content make it suitable for cooking. A native of central America, the plantain is usually larger than the banana and can be boiled, baked, fried or used to thicken soups.

Polenta   A corn meal pudding eaten as porridge or most often cooked then cooled, sliced and fried, grilled or baked. Polenta is a specialty of Venice and northern Italy where it is held in special regard.

Quinoa   The oldest grain known to man; quinoa dates back to the Aztec Indians. Quinoa comes close to achieving a perfect balance of essential amino acids, the building blocks of protein. Its protein is far higher than rice, corn or barley, it is high in lysine where most grains are low in this amino acid. Quinoa also has methionine and cystine, two amino acids that are low in most soybean varieties. Quinoa has been referred to as "the best source of protein in the vegetable kingdom" and is rich in vitamins, minerals and fiber.

Radicchio   A type of chicory with red or pinkish leaves. It can can used as a colorful addition to a salad or steamed as a vegetable.

Rice   A grain native to India and probably the world's most important food crop. In milling, removal of the hull produces brown rice. Removal of the bran and most of the germ produces unpolished rice. Converted rice has been steamed and dried before milling for higher nutritional content and easier processing. For more information on rice refer to page 110.

Rice Milk   An important replacement for dairy milk products, made from brown rice. Rice milk is a little sweeter than skim milk and comes in a variety of flavors. It is also available fortified with calcium and Vitamin D to replace the dairy nutrients.

Rice Vinegar This delicate flavored vinegar has about half the level of acid as cider vinegar. Brown rice vinegar has greater nutritional integrity. Rice vinegar can also be made from white rice and may contain additives.

Seitan A meat substitute also referred to as "wheat meat". Basically, seitan is a bread dough made from water and stone ground whole wheat flour. This wheat gluten protein is cooked in a soy sauce based broth and is fat-free. When cooked it has a texture that allows it to be substituted for cooked meat products, ranging from sliced and flavored deli-style products to larger pieces for stews .

Shoyu A naturally fermented soy sauce made from soy salt and wheat. It has a rich, complex flavor and is somewhat sweeter than tamari. It is more expensive than commercial soy sauce because of the the aging process and superior quality. Shoyu is best used in cold preparations of food.

Soba A buckwheat noodle prevalent in Asian cooking and available in Oriental and natural food stores.

Sofrito A mixture of chopped or pureed vegetables, peppers and herbs that can be simmered together with vinegar and or olive oil and used to season vegetables or meat.

Soy Milk A cholesterol-free replacement for dairy milk. It has about the same amount of protein , one third the fat, less calcium and fifteen times as much iron as cows milk products, with far less contaminents.

Spelt An ancient grain recently introduced in the U.S. An ancestor of modern hybrid wheat, most spelt is grown in Ohio and lesser amounts in Michigan and Indiana. Because spelt contains gluten, spelt flour can totally replace whole wheat in baking breads. Spelt is about 30 percent higher in protein than wheat and can be found in natural food stores in a variety of pastas or flour.

Sucanat Short for "sugar cane natural", Sucanat is probably the highest quality sweetener available. It is made by processing the juice from sugar cane. Sucanat is light in color like brown sugar, has a slight molasses flavor, and can be used in place of white sugar. Because it is not a fully refined product, Sucanat cannot be called sugar. It is also a rich source of potassium, calcium, magnesium, iron and carbohydrates. There is also a "Honey Sucanat " now available at most natural food stores.

Sweet Potato A root vegetable indigenous to Central America and brought back to Europe by Columbus. High in nutrients, the sweet potato actually has a lower glycemic index than the white potato. Often confused with the yam, especially in the U.S., the sweet potato has a reddish skin and a texture like the regular potato.

Tabbouleh   A Lebanese specialty mixing steamed bulgur with chopped tomatoes, onion, mint, parsley, lemon juice and olive oil.

Tahini   Simply stated "sesame butter", tahini is made from ground sesame seeds. Made popular in the Middle Eastern cuisine, tahini can be found in ethnic or natural food stores. It has an overwhelming flavor, somewhat limiting its use and popularity. Tahini is a good source of protein, low in saturated fat and it is not hydrogenated. At times the oil may separate from the ground seeds. Do not pour off the oil, simply re-blend it into the ground seeds. The oil serves as a natural protectant to retain moisture in the ground seeds.

Tamari   Tamari is the liquid that rises to the top when making soybean miso. It is naturally fermented in vats for three months and in some varieties up to one year. Tamari withstands intense heat much better than shoyu, which is another soybean product.

Tarragon   An herb from the daisy family made famous by the French. It is essential in Bearnaise Sauce, bouquet garni and is one of the "fines herbes".

Teff   An Ethiopian grain that has the distinction of being the smallest grain in the world. Rich in protein, iron and minerals, teff has almost twenty times the calcium of wheat or barley. It can be found as teff flour, cereal or in Ethiopian flatbread or instant seitan recipes.

Tempeh   Tempeh is made from soybeans or a variety of grains ranging from brown rice, to quinoa. It is infused with a bacteria culture that binds the soybeans and grains together in a thin loaf form. Tempeh is probably the richest protein food of all the soyfoods. It has as much protein per serving as beef or chicken and 50 percent more than hamburger. Because it is a fermented product, tempeh is easy to digest. One strong attraction tempeh has to vegetarians is its high content of vitamin B12, commonly thought unavailable in the vegetable kingdom. A four ounce serving of tempeh may have as much as 160 percent of the RDA for vitamin B12, and only 160 calories.

Thyme   A Mediterranean herb used in ancient times for medicinal purposes and an essential part of the "bouquet garni".

Tofu   Tofu is the white curd made from coagulated soymilk. Probably the most popular soyfood today, tofu is rich in protein, easily digestible and has been known to have many health benefits. For more information consult the Entrees chapter tofu section.

Tomatillo   A Mexican green tomato, that is small and pungent. It is not an unripe red tomato. Tomatillos are excellent raw, grilled or roasted, then added to salsas or salads.

Turmeric   A spice obtained from the dried and powdered rhizome of an Indian plant. Its bitter flavor and deep yellow color contribute to curries and can also serve as a natural food color, less expensive than saffron.

Umeboshi   Sour, immature plums that are fermented and salted with an herb known as beefsteak. The Japanese use it as a seasoning; others use it for medicinal purposes. Umeboshi vinegar has a fruity flavor, a cherry aroma and a purplish color. Because it contains salt, it technically is not a vinegar, but is excellent in salad dressings to replace other vinegars and salt.

Wakame   The most popular seaweed in Japan . Wakame can be found dried or fresh- packed with salt. To rehydrate dried wakame, place in warm water and when softened gently remove and place on a cutting surface. Trim and remove the outer stem and cut or chop the leaves for salads, miso soup or to season vegetables or rice. Wakame has more minerals and nutritional value than most land vegetables .

Wasabi   A plant often referred to as Japanese horseradish, whose root is used as a spice for sushi dishes. Pale green in color and very hot in flavor, wasabi comes fresh, powdered or in a paste. Its intense spice index has been known to cause a few tears to be shed when overused.

Wheat   A grain of world-wide importance because of its ability to form leavened bread when combined with yeast and water. There are many types of wheat flour. For maximum nutritional value use stoneground , whole wheat or durum semolina flours.

Wild Rice   A grass native to the Great Lakes region of North America and a distant cousin of rice. While rather expensive, wild rice is a staple Indian food, due to its high protein and carbohydrate values.

Yam   A tuberous vegetable, that is popular worldwide, due to its high protein and starch content. It has a white or yellowish flesh and brown skin. The yam is often confused in the U.S., where a variety of sweet potato is mistakenly called yam.

Yeast, Nutritional   A powdered product similar to brewers yeast, but not as bitter. Yeast is a tremendous source of protein and all the essential amino acids; the building blocks of protein for the body. Sprinkle over cereal, salads or in dressings and sauces for additional nutritional value. Vegans must be cautious when purchasing nutritional yeast. There are some brands that contain whey , a dairy by-product.

Index

*Vegetarian Kid's Favorites

258

Index

Vegetarian Kid's Favorites

Index

Vegetarian Kid's Favorite